Your Weaknesses Are Your Strengths

MONKS OF MT. TABOR

YOUR WEAKNESSES ARE
YOUR STRENGTHS

TRANSFORMATION OF THE SELF
THROUGH ANALYSIS OF PERSONAL WEAKNESSES

BY DAVID EDMAN
FOREWORD BY JOSEPH F. DOWNEY, S.J.

A Campion Book
LOYOLA UNIVERSITY PRESS
CHICAGO

Loyola University Press
3441 North Ashland Avenue
Chicago, Illinois 60657

Cover and interior design by Nancy Gruenke. Interior art by Mary O'Connor.

Library of Congress Cataloging-in-Publication Data
Edman, David.
    Your weaknesses are your strengths : transformation of the self through analysis of personal weaknesses / David Edman ; foreword by Joseph F. Downey.
       p. cm.
    Includes bibliographical references and index.
    ISBN 0-8294-0777-4
    1. Self-perception. 2. Self-evaluation. 3. Self-actualization (Psychology) I. Title.
BF697.5.S43E35 1994; aa21 09-03-93
158'.1--dc20   93-33156
                                            CIP

The poem "Walter Simmons" by Edgar Lee Masters is from *Spoon River Anthology,* originally published by Macmillan Company (New York, 1962). Used by permission of Ellen C. Masters.

The Bible text in this publication is from the *New Revised Standard Version of the Bible,* Division of Christian Education of the National Council of the Churches of Christ in the U.S.A., 1989, and is used by permission.

For my wife, Rita, and my brother, Victor

For when I am weak, then am I strong.

2 Corinthians 12:10

I was surprised to find myself so much fuller of faults than I had imagined.

Benjamin Franklin's *Autobiography*

Contents

Foreword

David Edman was intrigued that his manuscript had been accepted by Loyola University Press within a day of its receipt. Presumably, he had anticipated a delayed response allied with his own initial resistance to his findings.

It happens that Edman's premise runs parallel with a basic structure in the Ignatian spiritual way, namely, the advice to the aspiring pilgrim/Christian to "go against the self." For the most part, this means recognizing and coping not with one's strengths but with personal weaknesses.

Again, a time-honored staple of Ignatian method, the "Examen of conscience"—later amended to read examination of "consciousness"—is a daily short session of reflective prayer that relates well to Edman's directives on the need to explore personal failings close up and habitually. A companion directive is that the affective experience of desolation or put-down should always be included.

As the author suggests, a moral argument for undertaking such self-scrutiny may attract the reader: the process actually brings reliable growth and, eventually, true self-realization. In the Ignatian system, moreover, a further value takes place. To go forward may well take the faltering self into the mystery of his or her personal relationship with Christ. As the Gospel puts it: "The follower who loses his life for my sake will discover who he is." (Matt. 10:39)

Those drawn to make this pilgrimage beside a troubled self will find that the way is strewn with uncertainty and deception.

Eventually, it becomes clear that a purpose is working alongside, namely, to hone the pilgrim's purity of intention. At the same time, recurring ambiguities may suggest it is no place for the uninitiated. Thus, an experienced mentor such as David Edman and a commonsense method for coping with the ups-and-downs of the inner landscape will help considerably. In some cases, those who embrace this uphill course will have the advantage of a supportive community life-style. But if a religiously neutral context is indicated, the present pages represent an impressive beginning.

One can distinguish different levels of application, of course. The first level is more or less conventional, covering the problems and obstacles—usually in adolescence and the early adult years—that everybody faces. The commonly proposed answer is to accept, interiorly, the rule of the Ten Commandments or their equivalent, especially when including one's neighbor. Here the key to healthy answers is often found in the influence of significant others.

But a more interesting and subtle prospect can occur, say between the ages of thirty-five to forty. In those years the faith predicament is often solitary, and the faith-models we have followed no longer inspire confidence. Some have compared it to living spiritually "between systems"; a reigning moral code, for example, has become ineffective and a better founded spirituality has yet to take shape. This is where the lonely one-on-one encounter with the self can profit much from the wisdom, the method, and the rules set forth by the author. It will also profit to have had an early running start.

Joseph F. Downey, S. J.
Editorial Director
Loyola University Press

Introduction

The term *serendipity* implies a situation in which, while searching for a known item, a person happens upon something else, something infinitely more wondrous and valuable than that being sought.

In my case, I was perpetually on the lookout for better ways of helping those contemplating marriage to analyze the strengths and weaknesses that characterized their relationships. More than thirty years of premarital counseling had convinced me that an examination of the dynamics of bonding provided couples with far more practical and spiritual help than the usual clergy lectures about forbearance and attending church. As a result, I kept my eye out for ever more helpful techniques, the most successful to date being, in my estimation, the Minneapolis-based Prepare-Enrich program.

As it happened, one afternoon in the late 1980s when the path I then trod had turned a bit stony, it occurred to me that the process might be imposed on the self alone. What, I wondered, were my *own* strengths and weaknesses? How did they impinge on the difficulties I then faced?

I assumed I knew my strengths and weaknesses. To be sure, I never failed to be astonished by what seemed a peculiar blindness among those being given premarital counseling to the liabilities that threatened them. Only I was different . . . wasn't I? And yet, struggling with a host of vexations, it seemed to me that at least *some* examination of my assets and liabilities as a

human being might be of help. What, precisely, *were* those strengths that caused me to deal with life as I did? What, if any, my corresponding weaknesses? And to what extent did either of these bear on present problems?

Significant moments in one's life often resolve themselves into photographs of the mind. I turn a page of memory, and there to my inner eye appears the room where I began a half-hearted endeavor to catalog my personal strengths and weaknesses. A shaft of winter sunlight slants through the window. A yellow, lined legal pad rests on the desk as, with some bemusement, I marvel that a man in his mid-fifties seems to be admitting that there are certain aspects of his life he has not quite discovered yet. The project, I recall, struck me as faintly ludicrous. How could I know that I was about to find the prize that had eluded me all my life, or, more ironic still, that a great fortune was waiting to be found in a dark mine of unexamined weaknesses?

I began that afternoon by jotting down my strengths. Later I would discover, as I began to share this method with others, that those who were unusually depressed or defeated would characteristically begin by listing their weaknesses. Most—as in my case—however would turn immediately to those aspects of themselves that stand in the foreground: the abilities, assets, personality traits, and marketable skills that work best for them.

And why not? Humans tend to know where their strengths lie. If there be any doubt, our colleagues, managers, parents, teachers, and friends call attention to them constantly. Compliments, encouragement, thanks, praise resound frequently in our ears, even as there remains a general conspiracy of silence regarding our weaknesses. Five minutes and my list of personal strengths was complete.

My inventory of weaknesses, I confidently assumed, would be concluded in half the time. I'd never given them much thought. Nor, as mentioned, were they often referred to by others. So rarely, indeed, that I could almost count the times the cruel, factual truth was uttered and by whom—the exasperated teacher, the irate sergeant, the parent abruptly out of patience. We remember the cut, the festering infection, but chalk it up to something other than accuracy. Those who rail at us—we tell ourselves that there must be something wrong with *them!* They are momentarily out of focus. Blame it on a bad day, fatigue, PMS, *anything* but the cold, clear truth. And so we salve our feelings with pity for their distress, unctuously forgiving their unkindness while refusing the blessed possibility that the impatient assessments of those close to us, not to mention the insults and innuendos of our adversaries, can be the most generous gifts imaginable, if we but reach out and take them in our hands.

Here let us enter the melancholy truth, to be enlarged upon in the chapters that follow, that our entire emotional system is designed to deny personal weaknesses. To admit to them is not merely depressing; it is downright hazardous. Vulnerability implies danger. Who knows what will happen if those uneasy suspicions that lurk just beyond the borders of consciousness might prove true? And so, even as we assign our personal strengths a front-row-center status, our frailties and faults are kept out in the alley. Strengths are what matter. Strengths will see me through. Even if I *might* own up to a weakness or two, my abilities are more than a match for them.

Such was my confidence as I began a desultory search for the weaknesses that lay under a great mound of reassurances, assumptions, rationalizations, and avoidances. I felt certain they were few in number, inconsequential in substance.

I recall spending ten minutes with the debit column when a bout of fatigue overtook me. Wandering off in search of a cup of coffee, I next managed to think of some task that required urgent attention the remainder of that afternoon. It would be awhile before I came to recognize the tricks the unconscious plays when threatened.

Late the following afternoon I reviewed my entries. My list of strengths lay smug and content. But those few weaknesses I'd managed to jot down troubled me. They seemed much too vague, too evasive, too euphemistic. I took up my pen again. Before I got to wondering about a nap, I found yesterday's confidence—that my personal weaknesses were neither many nor influential—was turning a bit fluid. Where, I fretted, as one weakness begat another, were all those little devils coming from? Was there no end to them? Their variation as well as their capacity for permutation began to appall me. Before I finished that day, my list of weaknesses had overtaken my puny list of strengths threefold, fourfold, even fivefold.

A few grinding days later, I assumed my inventory was complete. All that remained was a process of distillation, which is to say, the reduction of my welter of entries to a few general concepts.

Wrong. My efforts at coalescence only suggested new possibilities. I found myself being forced to yet a second reconnaissance of the ground I'd been traversing, giving rise to the promise of yet more entries to come. I was reminded of the occasion on a Maine hillside when I was given a small blueberry patch to rake. Surveying the area, my eyes told me the most I could expect was a quart or so of the berries; by the time I'd finished, there stood two substantial cardboard boxes filled to capacity and almost too heavy to carry. Amazing how those tiny blue globes had so concealed themselves from my view.

"Curiouser and curiouser," said Alice. By rights this increasingly horrid inventory should have pitched me into a major depression. How could so many faulty parts constitute a machine that worked? By rights the thing belonged in the junkyard. Only such was not my reaction. Quite the opposite. I found myself overtaken by what I can only describe as a profound sense of release. No matter that the procedure itself was less than pleasant. At least I had gotten in touch with an identity that had eluded me all these years.

More astonishing still was an immediate transformation in my dealings with others. Sensing they discerned my weaknesses (a cardinal principle that will be discussed further along), I suddenly found myself able to interact with them in a more relaxed and honest manner than I had ever experienced. Why? Because having begun to see them *as they saw me,* I was rid of the obligation to forever be creating an impression. John Keats observed that all conversation was an attempt at effect.[1] His shrewdness stings, even as it suggests the extent to which our energies are absorbed by playacting. "So that is why people react to me the way they do," I began to tell myself as I experienced the shock of recognizing *my* weaknesses in *their* reactions.

My closer relationships, meanwhile, seemed to be undergoing a salutary change. One's behavior in the home takes the character of the habitual. Awareness of personal weaknesses had provided a new measure of control over bad domestic habits.

Indeed the entire universe seemed to be taking on new perspectives by means of a force I'd never before identified, though I had experienced its power many times in mutant forms. That force, I began to realize, is easily the most powerful means for personal change available to us, or so I shall argue in the final chapters of this book.

Meanwhile, I found a number of pernicious attitudes changing. One example was a transformed attitude toward my parents. No matter that they had been dead for some years; they
remained quite alive in the ordering of life, as psychologists are
wont to remind us. In a manner characteristic of our age, I had
settled into a negative mood toward them, one of blame for my
various failures. Surely *they* were at the root of my troubles.
Surely it was *their* mistakes that made me what I'd become.
Odd, is it not, the extent to which modern psychology enables
us to blame parents for our liabilities with hardly a nod in their
direction for our assets?

Now, suddenly, the old resentments were beginning to evap-
orate, replaced with what I can only describe as a new-found
sense of appreciation—yes, even love for them. Of course, I
continued to recognize those weaknesses that I had long ago
detected with all of the inborn skill by which we penetrate each
other's disguises. Only for the first time I began to realize what
a trial I had been to them, indeed experienced no little anger
toward myself for my jerky adolescent behavior, even as I felt
gratitude for their forbearance and patience. It occurred to me,
incidentally, that my own children had already summed me up
just as accurately. Had they come to blame me for life's debits?
Whatever my culpability, at least the understanding allowed
one granite *commendatore* to descend from his pedestal.

Trite though it may seem, the attitude beginning to emerge
through the cracks was a sense of responsibility for self. 'Tis a
concept foreign to an age that universally assumes that everyone else is to blame for one's condition and therefore imposes a
universal liability that, of course, stops short of the self. Whom
or what do I blame for *this?* we wonder as each new frustration
walks though the door. The approach is readily whipped into a
frenzy by those clever enough to exploit the power of grievance. *Grievance.* The bubonic pestilence of our era. Poor me. So
put upon. Even WASP males are beginning to feel sorry for
themselves. And what makes grievance so dangerous is that it
feels so good. Quite the opiate!

The distribution of blame is easily the greatest industry on
the face of the earth. Blame parents. Blame the government.
Blame social attitudes. Blame the other sex. Blame employers,
educators, physicians, majorities, the system. Only then, turn
blame into hard cash. Resort to litigation. Give grievance its

price tag. After all, there are juries literally slavering with eagerness to hand out millions. If litigation fails, then demand compensation by the system. Who cares if the government check breeds dependency. Just assume that one's fate must be the fault of something or someone else, and live off the proceeds.

Only in my case, as my list of personal weaknesses grew, I began to become cognizant of the extent to which my life had been blighted by doling out responsibility for those failings of which I was sole proprietor. Not that I was without precedent in the matter. After all, had not Adam and Eve set the pace? "*She* did it," were among the first words out of the human mouth, by the Bible's account. World population soars and with it the din of accusing voices: "*You* did it! *He* did it! *They* did it!" Blame truly is the world's leading enterprise. It is also the world's leading source of personal paralysis.

So there in the twilight of middle age I found myself beginning to recognize my own involvement in the prevalent insanity. Had the time at last come, I wondered, to accept the dignity of being author of my own mistakes, failures, evil deeds—yes, and accidents too? For even the misfortune of being struck by lightning usually reveals at least some slight lack of prudence. As for my more glaring indiscretions, it was becoming more difficult to say, "the devil made me do it," not to mention demon rum, society, ignorance, discrimination, parents, genes, circumstances. I was their author and their architect, contractor, bricklayer, and decorator—I, me, myself alone.

But why, I kept asking myself, why should this hideous recognition bring about elevation of spirit? Could it be true, that old scriptural paradox about the person humbling himself experiencing exaltation? Virtually everyone realizes by now that happiness has no front door. The welcome mat is somewhere out back. So, the doctor says to his new and very depressed patient, "You need to lighten up. Have a good laugh. Go to the circus and see Rimaldo the clown." Replies the patient: "I am Rimaldo."

It occurred to me, as I continued my investigation, that this expanding catalog of personal weaknesses was turning into something of a marathon confession. The nearest I'd come to anything resembling the process could be found in those old penitential manuals for examining conscience. That the practice of confession, both public and private, has gone into a steep decline indicates the mood of the age. Churches now emphasize "celebration." We need to compliment, not berate ourselves. Clergy are no longer confessors, but "celebrants" who ease away our vices. Only now I was beginning to realize, as never before, that the old practice of penitence might not be so much a registry of errors as a liberating admission of *who*, in fact, I was!

And yet, even as my spirits rose, my chafed ego roused itself too. All of this navel-gazing, what did it come to beyond a new manifestation of self-absorption? *Acceptance* of self was the solution, not scruple-mongering. Still, how can one accept the unidentified? How can one affirm that which stands hidden in the shade? My response was to come down with a good case of "yes—buts." Yes, that might be true of me, *but* —— . . .

Still, somewhere I managed to find the power to persist and fitfully began at last to emerge from the silken cocoon of the illusions and rationalizations that had hitherto deeded me to a sort of half-life.

The road proved lonely. I spoke to no one of my endeavors. The reason? It began with the unwillingness to admit vulnerabilities. But then came an intimation that later proved good; namely, that the road being described here must be a solitary one. The moment it veers into those realms of chatter about self that pose as therapy, the spell of inner integrity becomes broken.

Even as the continental plates were beginning to move, I found myself wondering if the experience might work for others. We bang our heads against the door lintel every morning for fifty years, then discover that by either wearing a helmet or stooping a bit a great deal of pain could have been avoided. Only will someone else benefit from the insight?

I had not long to wait. Into my office one morning came my secretary. With a despairing glance toward heaven, she whispered that one of my regulars had arrived demanding immediate admission. There was no option. In strode a woman looking more cross and determined than usual. Fixing me with a steely eye, she came directly to the point. She was divorcing her husband and . . . that was that. No sense trying to dissuade her. She'd made the appointment with her lawyer. Her visit to my office was merely a formality.

As if I needed more evidence of her determination, she proceeded to launch into yet another attack upon her husband. He was ignorant. He was lazy. He was inconsiderate. He had no ambition. He was an incompetent provider and parent.

In fact, she was speaking of someone I did not even recognize. The husband who I knew was, by any reasonable assessment, an intelligent and agreeable sort who worked two jobs to make ends meet and spent much of his spare time at home fixing up the house. Indeed, how he could tolerate the abuse that had been his lot for most of their marriage could only be accounted for by an extraordinarily pacific temperament, not to mention a genuine love for his wife that defied her best attempts to kill it.

I had tried to extol her husband in the past, but nothing, I could see, would be gained on that front today. Neither would scriptural cautions about divorce, nor reference to the practical consequences of divorce upon the family budget. Here was a woman in no mood to be talked out of anything!

Only on this day another arrow lay in my quiver. When at last I was able to slip in a few words, I asked a favor. Reminding her that I had spent many hours discussing her problems, that I had provided referrals, and even paid the fees of various therapists, I told her that in my opinion she *owed* me a favor.

The woman regarded me darkly. What sort of favor did I have in mind?

As simply as I could, I asked that before proceeding with the divorce she take fifteen minutes a day for the next few weeks to assemble a list of personal weaknesses. The rules of the procedure I explained briefly. No one was to be told of what she was doing, neither before, during, nor after the process. When the list was complete, I wanted her to destroy it and never to speak to anyone of it, not even me. If afterward she decided to go ahead and divorce her husband, she could be assured of my pastoral support.

Her immediate response was characteristic. She told me that she knew very well what her weaknesses were. Couldn't I see that the problem was her *husband's* weaknesses, not her own? I responded by saying that before taking a closer look, I, too, had assumed I had known my weaknesses, but in fact I hadn't.

What possible help, she demanded to know, could she expect of such shenanigans? And besides, her lawyer was expecting to see her that very afternoon. I could think of no response. I only reiterated that perhaps she owed me a favor, and on that basis she gave a reluctant consent.

I caught sight of her at various church functions over the next few weeks, but there was no indication whatsoever that she had followed through on my suggestion. For all I knew, the lawyer was preparing the documents.

Then, one morning, almost two months later, came a tap at my office door. Outside stood this woman, with a letter in her hand. Ordinarily a voluble person, she asked only that I read what she had written, then turned and left.

The letter remains in my files. It is an extraordinary document of a mighty transformation at all levels of a person's life. What's more, in the months to come I began to watch as a marriage in tatters turned into a situation more resembling a honeymoon. The body language told it all. Not only had the two begun to *look* at each other, but they did so with such longing and tenderness they might have been Romeo and Juliet.

Since that time I have based my pastoral counseling almost solely on a preliminary investigation of personal weaknesses. Counselees tend to be surprised by a pastor whose response to their concerns is not so much compassion and Bible verses as the suggestion they initiate an inventory of personal flaws. It is out of such experiences that this work has emerged, a book about the transformation of the self through the analysis of personal weaknesses.

I have attempted to set forth the material in a clear, logical fashion, beginning with an explanation of why it is so important to overcome an innate tendency to disregard personal liabilities. It concludes with an uncomplicated method for cataloging them. The very process puts one in possession of what I believe to be the most powerful agent for change that exists: *there is no more swift or certain way to inner, social, and spiritual integration than the identification and acknowledgment of personal liabilities.*

These introductory words would not be complete without the admission that there is nothing new about the principles that animate this work. Most are older than recorded history, appearing full-blown in earliest folklore and myth throughout the world. In time they came to provide the basics of classical philosophy and later served as accepted postulates of theology and psychology, inasmuch as both disciplines regard the cognitive recognition of inner dysfunction as indispensable to the integration of the self. That they stand at the center of Scriptures goes without saying.

As well grounded as these principles may be, however, the human race seems grimly determined to act and believe otherwise, supposing against all argument and experience that personal strengths, or the illusion thereof, can overcome all. It is with this persuasive and pervasive delusion, incidentally, that one may find the reason for the popularity of that cultural American phenomenon known as "positive thinking." The belief that an exalted view of the self combined with boundless optimism can serve as an effectual means of dealing with life's adversities is typical of American buoyancy. But like Professor Harold Hill's "think method" for learning music—Hill was a major character in the film *The Music Man*—it holds no more than a surface plausibility. Any system of self-betterment that fails to take seriously the determinative influence of personal weaknesses upon the destiny of each human being is surely one that will inevitably fail.

Our approach rather follows the path of a wholesome pessimism and to a certain extent could even be called "the power of negative thinking." Fundamental to our argument is the absolute necessity for examining those areas of life we would sooner forget. And yet the way down remains the way up; the way in, the way out. Anyone who seriously analyzes personal liabilities cannot fail to be changed—though "changed" may not be the best word, rather "changing" is much preferred. For as the self recognizes its limitations and begins to shed its harmful pretenses, as strengths become subject to the control of realistic self-perception, life in all of its richness and potential will be experienced as never before—an assurance to which the author can personally attest.

1

Your Weaknesses Are Your Strengths

The pages that follow rest upon a simple premise. The key to self-fulfillment lies with a comprehensive recognition and admission of personal weaknesses.

This premise further implies that it remains within the capacity of most persons to undertake, without assistance, a systematic investigation of personal weaknesses. Such weaknesses may be congenital in nature or the consequence of circumstances. They may have been imposed from without or adopted consciously or unconsciously as a means of compensatory behavior. Whatever their source, the recognition and admission of these personal weaknesses can provide a powerful first step in the transformation of the self toward its true potential.

The Hiddenness of Personal Weaknesses

People *assume* awareness of their deficiencies. "I know my faults," is a familiar refrain. However, it would be truer to say that we humans are quite blind to our weaknesses—and insist on remaining so. In many respects we are total strangers to ourselves, a point that will be elaborated further along.

As a consequence, any realistic discernment of the weaknesses that vitiate our lives requires a deliberate, conscious, systematic effort. Such self-investigation will invariably prove uncomfortable, since it will bring revelations that are not altogether pleasant. Nevertheless, the scalpel wounds in order to heal. If self-assessment begins with the bad, the good soon overtakes it as a sense of authentic selfhood emerges and creative energies become unleashed by a realistic awareness of the self's true status.

The Personal Weaknesses Inventory

Various means for discerning personal liabilities have been put forward over the years. The concluding chapters of this book describe yet another. We call it a *Personal Weaknesses Inventory*. In a broad sense, there is nothing novel about the Inventory. Its procedures are common to both applied psychology and practical religion, which is to say it shares similarities both with standard psychotherapeutic techniques and traditional means of examining conscience as set forth in manuals of penitence. It is, however, the *integration* of contemporary psychological insights and established forms of penitential self-examination that are combined here as a means of personal transformation for those who, for one reason or another, have failed to gain a purchase on life.

We must acknowledge at the outset that the theoretical underpinnings of the Personal Weaknesses Inventory and the accompanying discussion rely heavily on the traditional Christian "doctrine of man," in particular the assertion that the root of human misery is found in the tendency of mortals to assume they are gods, even as they patently suffer the conditions of their mortality.

Pride (*hubris*) remains the single most influential component in the makeup of the self. We tend to swagger through life, even though the pride that prompts this ordinarily has a way of degenerating into comedy or tragedy. By contrast, the humble recognition of limitation and failure, that seems such a step downward, paradoxically, provides the only possible means of ascent.

While animated by a Christian orientation, the approach suggested here, with its requirement of a secluded, unassisted cataloging of personal weaknesses, can be readily adapted by those of alternative faith systems, or none at all. However characterized, however directed, the work of contrition provides a powerful impulse for new direction in life. The term *repentance* (*metanoia*) suggests a "turning-around." Our emphasis in this work is to declare that interior revolution requires first an accurate understanding of what one is turning from. One must become cognitively aware of life's limitations and failures. Such awareness may be discomfiting, yet it points the way to new and more hopeful vistas.

In short, while proceeding from Christian presuppositions, our approach should not be regarded as an enclosed religious system. Rather, it is one that can be universally applied as corresponding also with the broad principles of psychology and western philosophy.

We would further add that a systematic cataloging of personal weaknesses can prove beneficial across the entire range of spiritual and emotional conditions. Even those who consider themselves reasonably healthy can find in the Personal Weaknesses Inventory a source of enormous personal enrichment. Though the results may not seem overly dramatic, the Inventory can provide a measure of ethical ennoblement and refinement of life goals.

Far more spectacular results may be experienced by those suffering the anxiety-depressive symptoms that come of deeply-rooted neuroses or character disorders. For these individuals, the Inventory can provide a number of "first steps," among them the very recognition of a need for professional psychotherapeutic treatment.

To be sure, any effort at self-scrutiny is bound to stir the inner furies. *Resistance* will paradoxically serve as the best indication that the Inventory is doing its healing work. Resistance, we would advise at the outset, must in turn be resisted.

The investigation of the self must take into account the fact that humans ordinarily shield themselves from their personal weaknesses by elaborately-contrived defense systems.[1] These commonly take the form of various posturings intended to display the appearance of invincibility. Far too often such displays turn into the illusory strengths that, as we shall point out in the following chapter, can prove our greatest weaknesses. To the extent that the illusory has some basis in truth, these very weaknesses can be transformed into useful strengths as long as they are fully discerned and acknowledged.

Most readers will recognize that the defenses we contrive for the protection of the ego function as both shield and prison. In order to break out of a prison, one must forego the security of its encircling walls. The Personal Weaknesses Inventory provides the incidental benefit of indicating the extent to which our defenses are in fact dungeons, not castles as supposed. A cursory reflection on the lives of those who surround us—neighbors, colleagues, relatives—reveals that most people go through life unaware that they inhabit prisons of their own devising. Alas, what we presume of others, we rarely suspect of ourselves. Again, the Personal Weaknesses Inventory will make plain the nature of our personally customized confinement. As noted, the revelation will initially raise anxiety levels and beckon despair, for we imagine that the protection is worth the liabilities. Gradually, however, the glory inherent in personal liberty will begin to manifest itself, and fearfulness will at last be revealed as only another set of shackles.

In such a transition, the Christian will take heart in the redemptive power of the God who delivered Israel from its chains, claiming also with the Apostle: "For freedom Christ hath set us free."[2] For those of little or no religious persuasion, there can be the reminder that the path to personal liberty is, at the very least, an adventure worth the taking.

The determination to "break out" of self-imposed prisons certainly remains an option for every human being. To those prepared to take the necessary risks is offered the promise that whatever emotional discomfort may be entailed, anxieties will eventually yield as one develops a new sense of the self, cleansed of all need for useless defensive redoubts.

More importantly, new life vistas will begin to manifest themselves the moment the walls are breached, even though it may be years before the significance of so daring an "escapade" is fully realized. The long-term consequences may be described in the Psalmist's phrase as a moving "from strength to strength,"[3] as illusory securities are abandoned and vulnerability is accepted as a necessary element in pressing on toward life's goals.

The Inherent Weakness of "Positive Thinking"

Resting as it does on the premise that conscious awareness of personal weaknesses constitutes the necessary ingredient in the fulfillment of the self, this work may seem, at first glance, an exercise in the obvious. And yet, self-evident though the presupposition may seem, the principle remains curiously elusive.

The human race continues its love affair with the opposing assumption: namely, that the recognition of personal strengths, accompanied by a disregard of personal weaknesses, holds the formula of self-fulfillment. This countertheory has proved itself not only more congenial but far more marketable as may be observed in those twin schools of self-improvement known as "positive religion" and "American optimism," with their can-do emphases. Along with cookbooks and diet manuals, best-seller lists invariably contain the latest prescription by which "attitude" can overcome personal deficiencies in the pursuit of success. Virtually all these systems are based upon the Peale/ Carnegie principle that an uncritical confidence in one's strengths, real or imagined, shows the way forward.

It is not the intent of this book to fashion a polemic against positive-thinking forms of self-help. Nevertheless, if we are to point out that the way to strength lies *through* the recognition and admission of personal liabilities, we must also recognize the pitfalls of a system that deals with life's negativities by dismissing them. At issue here, incidentally, is not a cheerful or hopeful disposition, which under any circumstances is to be preferred to its glum alternative. Rather we challenge the notion that by merely accentuating the positive and eliminating the negative personal success will be assured—a suggestion not far removed from that which counsels one to wish upon a star.

The Power of Negative Thinking

This book thus challenges the postulates of positive religion by affirming that it is only through a prior and undistorted examination of life's negativities that true progress can be achieved. Note again that the track being suggested here is not pessimism. It is often assumed that the alternative to optimism is pessimism. In fact, there is but one alternative to both optimism and pessimism: realism. François de La Rochefoucauld's epigram to the effect that either choice does not fully reflect the reality of the human situation ("*On n'est jamais si hereux ni si malheureux qu'on s'imagine*") puts the matter very well.[4] Chasing dreams has no advantage over being chased by nightmares.

Penitence as Therapy

In its orthodox mode, Christianity has stressed that the first step in redemption involves serious self-assessment. It is not enough to give weakness and failure a vague recognition. Specifics are required. One must engage in a defined, comprehensive acknowledgment of fault and folly if *salvation* is to be experienced—a term, incidentally, that is etymologically linked to "health" and "wholeness."

The point is well-expressed in C. S. Lewis's autobiography *Surprised by Joy,* as the author describes the necessaries surrounding his conversion. "For the first time I examined myself with a seriously practical purpose," he wrote. "And there I found what appalled me: a zoo of lusts, a bedlam of ambitions, a nursery of fears, a harem of fondled hatreds. My name was legion."[5]

Informed penitence as a precondition to empowerment is also consonant with the basic tenets of modern psychotherapeutic theories, with their insistence that integration of the ego lies by way of conscious recognition of inappropriate attitudes and behavior. The process invariably requires dissection of illusion, not its promotion, as tends to be the case with positive-attitude theories. We may be reminded here that philosophy too, at least in its classical forms, has regarded the path to life's fulfillment as commencing with self-scrutiny, reflected in the Delphic dictum to "know thyself," surely a principle at one with the Christian summons to repentance.

Positive thinking, like aspirin, may possess certain analgesic properties. But these will prove temporary, for in essence "attitude adjustment" constitutes a form of pretending—a point amusingly reflected in a possibly apocryphal story about Émile Coué, the nineteenth-century apostle of attitude therapy ("Every day in every way I'm getting better and better"). When an acquaintance reported the illness of an uncle, Coué waved off the possibility. "Don't say he's ill! Say he *thinks* he's ill!" A few weeks later Coué inquired about the uncle's condition only to be told: "He thinks he's dead."

The Denial of Weakness

We now turn our attention to the powerful, inborn human tendency to deny and conceal personal weaknesses. The roots of this human characteristic must be examined if we are to fully appreciate the necessity for the Personal Weaknesses Inventory.

We hardly need muster arguments to prove that humans characteristically conceal weaknesses behind an orchestrated display of invincibility and personal superiority. We observe the tendency in others and occasionally detect its presence in our own lives.

The usual means of concealing weaknesses is the creation of what Tournier calls a "personage."[6] The personage (or persona, as it is sometimes called) is what we want others to believe ourselves to be. Perhaps the most curious aspect of the trait is that we ourselves tend to become the first and most credulous believers in the idealized image we try to project.

While the human instinct to create a facade for the self is universal, its failure is similarly so. Rodney Dangerfield's plaintive "I don't get no respect" refers to the implausible personage that he himself implicitly accepts, even if no one else seems able to do so. His phrase strikes a resonating chord because all human beings experience the inevitable failure of performance. One's projected image never gets the acclaim it presumably deserves.

Enter at this point the human affinity for mood-altering chemicals. Why this compulsive fondness for the effects of, say, ethyl alcohol on the control centers of the brain, if not for its bolstering of the personage? The resort to alcohol and other drugs must be understood as having a basic drive, chiefly the power to deny weakness while providing the illusion of mastery. In other words, substances that release ego control seem to, above all, offer self-credibility. The purpose of inebriation is not so much to feel good, but rather to feel invincible. One becomes all one supposes oneself to be, despite sobriety's indications to the contrary.

In John Updike's *Rabbit at Rest,* the ineffectual son of the protagonist describes to his mother the rationale for his cocaine addiction: "After a hit, I feel no pain. I guess that means I feel pain the rest of the time. Everything is more intense, and more hopeful. . . . " Later he explains the power it imparts to his car-selling ability. "You can do a line at work quick in the john and nobody can tell the difference, except you feel like Superman. Sell like Superman, too. When you *feel* irresistible, you're hard to resist."[7]

Denial of Weaknesses as an Instinct

What are the forces that impel us to deny the weaknesses that, unacknowledged, consign us to lives of shadow and failure? A primary factor may reside deeply in the natural instincts. During the long evolutionary process, the human species was conditioned to adapt and compete on the basis of *strengths*. Just as animals "posture" in order to survive, we humans share with them the same protective mechanisms of intimidation so as to assure for ourselves a place in the sun.

Presentation of strengths necessarily involves concealment of weaknesses. One confronts another with an array of effects unconsciously designed to obtain superiority, or, failing that, at least parity. Among these are intimidation, seductiveness, the creation of confusion, and so forth. If required, animals will acknowledge their being overpowered with a display of submission, as when a dog, tail between its legs, rolls over on its back in the face of overwhelming odds. Humans, with a far greater range of resources, may similarly surrender, and yet go on to persuade themselves that they at least attained a "moral victory," so powerful is their need to deny weakness.

Parental Reinforcement of the Posturing Instinct

The instinctual tendency to present strengths while denying weaknesses becomes reinforced among humans during the nurturing process. Spurred by deep impulses to preserve the gene pool, parents train their children in the arts of survival by urging them to capitalize on inherited assets. Thus the alert child is encouraged to excel in school, the child with a talent for music is sent to the piano teacher, and the coordinated child is directed toward athletics.

An opposite tack is taken when one's inheritance of talents is deficient. If the coordinated child receives parental approval for competitive sports, the awkward child will be assured that athlet-

ics are for stupid people and promptly steered toward compensating pursuits. While beautiful children are made aware of their
advantages and trained to exploit them, unattractive children
will be taught that beauty is only skin deep and directed toward
compensatory forms of self-presentation. It is a rare parent who
can lovingly and wisely assist a child of mediocre gifts (or worse)
to confront his or her weaknesses, admit them, and attempt to
overcome them on the basis of accurate self-assessment.

Indeed, the more prevalent tendency is for parents to rein-
force the denial of weaknesses by ridicule or punishment.
Rather than help the plain child, the stuttering child, the slow
child, the obese child, or the child with a physical or mental
disability acknowledge and sublimate limitations, parents will
often intimidate them into compensating behaviors that prove
far worse than the original weakness. Bullies and braggarts are
commonly the result of parental attempts to shame away
inborn liabilities. The "runt" of the family may be repudiated
altogether, left to face life with overpowering feelings of worthlessness and subsequent suicidal tendencies.

These forces are unconscious and biologically programmed
throughout the organic chain. The survival instincts that
prompt higher primates to ignore their less-abled progeny,
even to the point of leaving them to starve to death, are fully
alive in humans as well. Few parents will actually abandon dys-
functional offspring. Nevertheless, they can send forth signals
of rejection powerful enough to affect infants during preverbal
stages of development. One theory suggests that autistic
children, who as a class seem to share an unusually high
intelligence, may be the victims of subtle parental rejection.
Retreating into defensive postures that protect the ego, such as
in schizophrenia, is, for others, their only defense.

Social Reinforcement of the Instinct

Finally, the encouragement to capitalize on strengths while
denying weaknesses is reinforced by a broad range of social attitudes. In western democracies, it is assumed that one's talents
constitute the most marketable aspect of the self. Education is
oriented toward the maximization of one's intrinsic talents.
Liabilities, on the other hand, tend to be partitioned off in such

a manner that they do not interfere with "success." Gurus of commerce thus suggest ways of "swimming with the sharks," even as popular religious leaders urge positive thinking to overcome those liabilities that are inherent or self-inflicted. Rarely is it suggested that personal weaknesses directly challenged may be the most crucial factor in the self's drive toward fulfillment.

Thus the concealment of weakness, implanted by survival instincts and augmented by parental and social attitudes, becomes a fixed perspective by the onset of adult years. Nature and nurture conspire to establish attitudes of denial about personal liabilities that leave too many people facing their productive years with misplaced confidence in illusory strengths, their life compass some 180 degrees off course. For them the only alternative to being lost in a sea of unrealistic assumptions is a cognitive identification of personal weaknesses.

We argue that the means thereof are readily at hand. The process is no quick fix, as promised by the win-through-attitude apostles. It begins with a degree of discomfort and never truly ends. But its undertaking provides the impetus for a personal liberation that ultimately brings a person to a new understanding of what genuine "success" is all about, as well as a realistic means of achieving it.

2

PRINCIPLE

Your Strengths Are Your Weaknesses

A second principle that demonstrates the need for a full, detailed comprehension of one's personal weaknesses involves the manifold vulnerabilities that lurk unseen and menacing in one's very strengths. Indeed it could be argued that a person's talents pose a far greater threat to the self's potential than a person's weaknesses.

Does Self-scrutiny Lead to Lowered Self-esteem?

Before taking up the implications of this principle, however, we must pause briefly in order to deal with an issue that has doubtless formed in the minds of many readers: namely, will a systematic analysis of personal weaknesses, such as that prescribed by the Personal Weaknesses Inventory, lower self-esteem? Granted that the truth about oneself may hurt, but will it also rouse the demons of self-doubt and despair?

When the Personal Weaknesses Inventory was in its initial stages of development, I asked a number of acquaintances to undertake the Inventory on an experimental basis. After describing its objective, I found, to my surprise, a considerable number who declined for the reasons cited above. One declared that she was only too aware of her weaknesses and did not need to be reminded of them. Said another: "Why should I dwell on the negative things about my life when I'm already on a guilt trip?" And yet a third replied, "Why should I do something that will only make me feel more worthless than ever?"

Ironically, such comments illustrate the very need for a systematic investigation of personal weaknesses. Low self-esteem tends to derive from a distorted evaluation of the self, an attitude that is incapable of distinguishing genuine shortcomings from the imputed variety ordinarily generated by the experiences of childhood. In other words, those oppressed by a negative self-image almost invariably *accuse themselves of the wrong things.* They are victims of a spectral self-condemnation that bears little relation to reality.

The only effective antidote to such oppression is accurate self-accusation. A clearheaded tally of failings may entail an initial dose of discouragement, as one surveys the actualities of one's condition. But surely this is to be preferred to endless and misplaced self-deprecation. A high percentage of people whose egos are battered by feelings of inadequacy suffocate under a cloud of undifferentiated guilt. This guilt robs them of the very capacity to identify those shortcomings that are not only real but also amenable to change through a process of awareness and admission that can ultimately transform weaknesses into strengths.

It is well known that pervasive feelings of guilt are primarily the residue of negative self-images imposed during childhood. Overly critical or demanding parents intensify the faculty of self-judgment that Freud termed the *superego,* which can be defined as the internalized parent capable of condemning a person to a perpetual sense of worthlessness. One can work and work and work toward achievement, but the *superego* automatically programs the capacity for self-acceptance to recede at the same pace as one's approach. "Give guilt," a comedienne once advised parents, "the gift that lasts."

Like a low-grade fever, a pervasive sense of failure can consign one to an equally pervasive state of helplessness that, existing just below the threshold of actual awareness, locks one into endless dejection. Much depression, even the clinical variety, can be broken, I am convinced, by a forthright, inner-generated assessment of the actuality of one's assets and liabilities. One may learn that he or she may not be so promising as imagined; but then, one may also discover that he or she is not so bad as feared.

Self-defeating Defenses against Low Self-esteem

The fate of the guilt-ridden is to erect protective redoubts against imposed feelings of shame or inadequacy. The problem is that the defenses often prove far more damaging to the self than the emotions that brought them about in the first place. For example, a common compensation for low self-esteem is a countering tendency to deny *all* personal weakness, imagining oneself to be "superior" or "special," and thus above any need to struggle and strive.

The result is a grandiose but unrealistic sense of personal abilities that, in turn, breeds an unhealthy hypersensitivity to any criticism that might call such self-delusion into question. One of the major difficulties with this particular defense strategy is the extent to which the consequent airs of superiority it fosters stir negative reactions in others that, in turn, only intensify the self-protective response. The result may be described as a particularly mean dog chasing its own well-bitten tail.

Thus, it might be asked, what better way to come to terms with nebulous self-accusation and its consequences than by a straightforward, rational identification of one's actual weaknesses? Granted again, such a procedure is not without its pangs. But one of its incalculable rewards will be the reduction of inappropriate self-accusation and punishment. What's more, a calculated examination of the self will point up the poignant irony in those piteous, self-reproaching litanies that say "I'm no good! I never do anything right! I'm a failure! I don't deserve to be alive!" The harboring of such self-depreciation may then be regarded as being *itself* a weakness that can yield to a grace-assisted effort at change. Truly, nothing so obscures the truth about the self more than self-loathing.

It is on the basis of such an understanding that we can dismiss the fear that cognitive investigation of personal weakness will lower self-esteem. Quite the contrary. Discernment is the way to *release*. We can confidently turn aside all self-protecting objections to an inventory of personal weakness with the biblical promise that the purpose of acknowledging one's liabilities is not to feel guilty about them but rather to enlist the various graces by which they may be *overcome.* The Lord's assurance to the woman taken in adultery is his promise to all: "Neither do I accuse thee; go and sin no more."

MONKS OF MT. TABOR

Unlike Weaknesses, Our Strengths Are Very Well Known to Us

We have previously noted the extent to which most people remain unaware of their weaknesses. We have argued that in order to gain conscious knowledge of personal liabilities, as well as *some* idea of their adverse effect upon our lives, there can be no option to the undertaking of some program of systematic identification.

We have further suggested that an effort of this nature can be self-generated. Despite all possibility of self-deception, the best judge of oneself remains . . . *oneself.* Why? In part because second-person judgments rouse self-protective stratagems that interfere with the ability to view oneself clearly. Be it parent, colleague, boss, spouse, or therapist the moment another person begins to identify your weaknesses, the immediate response is *defensiveness.* One may seem to welcome the evaluation of others, but acceptance is quite another matter. *Constitutionally, we resist criticism.* We wonder who can be more detestable than those who feel called upon to tell us truths about ourselves "for our own good." We suspect hostility to be their underlying motive and assure ourselves that "they don't know the real me," even as we dismiss their comments as little more than incoming enemy fire.

At this point, then, we can introduce yet another factor into our preliminary consideration of the Personal Weaknesses Inventory—personal strengths. We postulate the following: *to the same degree that humans tend to be ignorant of their personal weaknesses, they are commensurately aware of their strengths.*

Surely every Jack, Jill, and Johnny knows "where my talents lie." We know our capacities if for no other reason than the fact that we have been constantly reminded of them since earliest days. Parents, relatives, teachers, counselors, and friends are always ready to point out our potentialities, even as they politely overlook our faults.

One of the more fascinating aspects of biographies is the manner in which people of fame and fortune became aware of their strengths during earliest years. The catalyst for these strengths usually turns out to have been a significant adult, most often a mother, who managed to bring together those two ingredients crucial to success: inherent strengths and motivation.

The Hazards of Personal Strengths

Strengths come in a broad array of forms. Inherited wealth or station is certainly a strength. Intelligence, beauty, brawn, coordination, robust health, location of birth, quality of parenting, opportunity—these and many more may be accounted as inherent strengths.

Although made aware of those assets that form a part of the "givenness" of life, we tend to find ourselves oblivious to the hazards they entail. The Puritans, with their Calvinistic doctrine of "total depravity," recognized as clearly as anyone the double-edged character of one's talents and continuously cautioned their offspring about the temptations that accompany life's advantages. *The New England Primer* is full of warnings against placing confidence solely in ability or possessions. By contrast, today's climate urges upon children an uncritical acceptance of personal assets. Contemporary parents consider their marketability but rarely the perils they entail, as from nursery onward they directly or indirectly guide their children toward lucrative careers that interface with aptitude. Not that parents should be faulted for helping their offspring identify strengths and direct their application. Rather we suggest that effort be balanced by some fairly realistic appraisal of the extent of those talents, together with judicious warning about the jeopardy involved.

Overestimating and Underestimating Personal Strengths

Here we observe that being aware of inborn abilities and aptitudes does not necessarily insure a realistic appraisal of their comparative worth. Doting parents often impose grotesquely inflated estimates of their children's abilities, as, for example, imagining them to be Mozarts-in-the-making despite tin ears or candidates for the Heisman trophy though endowed with the congenital physique of a mouse. Such children may be uncritically praised for modest endeavors and thereby saddled with unrealistic self-expectations. As they grow older, they will then be conscious of their presumed strengths but puzzled as to why others don't seem to be aware of them.

In his *Spoon River Anthology,* Edgar Lee Masters describes such a case. Walter Simmons is the name engraved on the tombstone. This is the story he tells:

> My parents thought that I would be
> As great as Edison or greater:
> For as a boy I made balloons
> And wondrous kites and toys with clocks
> And little engines with tracks to run on
> And telephones of cans and thread.
> I played cornet and painted pictures,
> Modeled in clay and took the part
> Of the villain in "Octoroon."
> But then at twenty-one I married
> And had to live, and so, to live
> I learned the trade of making watches
> And kept the jewelry store on the square,
> Thinking, thinking, thinking, thinking,—
> Not of business, but of the engine
> I studied the calculus to build.
> And all of Spoon River watched and waited
> To see it work, but it never worked.
> And a few kind souls believed my genius
> Was somehow hampered by the store.
> It wasn't true. The truth was this:
> I didn't have the brains.[1]

The danger of overestimating strengths is mirrored by the equally dangerous tendency to <u>underestimate</u> them. A poignant example of the two existing side by side may be found in various accounts of the marriage of Scott and Zelda Fitzgerald. As insanity began to consume her, Zelda became obsessed with the belief that she was destined to be a great dancer. She would rehearse endlessly the same routine to the same melody played relentlessly, hour after hour on a Victrola. Her husband, meanwhile, seemed intent on misapplying his manifest abilities upon magazine and movie trifles. Edna St. Vincent Millay described him as resembling an ugly old woman possessed of a priceless diamond, yet unsure of what to do with it.

Without realistic evaluation of the true extent of one's strengths they will, like unused or misused muscles, deteriorate into flaccidity. Talents may go on being *claimed* by a process of conceit ("I'm potentially better than everyone else —"), even as they gradually dwindle to a point beyond all retrieval. Alternatively, they can be wistfully resigned, leaving their former possessor to a perpetual and melancholy speculation of "what might have been."

Blessed is the person who recognizes his abilities for what they are, for he will find himself. Many years ago in Rochester, New York, I found myself in conversation with a young man who was completing a degree at the Eastman School of Music in the field of music education. At that time he was planning to become a teacher at the secondary level, though later he settled on a career as a clergyman.

Neither had been his goal at matriculation, however. He'd come from a small Texas town where, as a teenager, he managed to become the most competent organist for miles around. He graduated from high school to choruses of praise and a fistful of awards, then went on to the college level in the certainty that this would be the final step before universal acclaim. Only when he arrived at Eastman, he found himself merely one in a company of organ students, most of whom were far more talented than he.

The jolt was considerable. He fell into a depression that left him totally incapable of either practice or study. Instead he took to sitting in the Eastman Theatre day after day, listening to various orchestras and ensembles rehearse. Only by degrees was he able to reevaluate his genuine but limited talents. At the end of his first semester, he changed his major from performance to education, thereby enabling himself to move forward in a positive frame of mind.

The Greatest Danger: Strengths That Succeed

The Greeks assigned to their goddess, Nemesis, the task of preventing any mortal from achieving absolute success. Not even the gods could be assured as much. Thus fortune would be forever shadowed by failure, prowess would have its Achilles heel;

the closer one flew to the sun the more vulnerable one's mode of flight, the higher one's ascent the more meteoric and swift the fall.

This mythological insight cannot fail to strike a resonant chord. Who, reading these words, will not call to mind a myriad of people whose strengths contributed directly to personal collapse: the intellectual who succumbed to Faustian temptation; the comely woman whose beauty became her undoing; or the silver-spooned heir who "had it all," yet ended in bankruptcy, disgrace, and prison—for, as Andrew Carnegie once commented, the almighty dollar bequeathed to children often turns out to be "the almighty curse."

An entire class of literature deals with the phenomenon. The customary term is *tragedy*. And what is tragedy? From ancient Greek dramatists to Shakespeare to contemporary playwrights, tragedy is that genre of narrative that tracks the destiny of a particular human being who relies on personal strengths to overcome the forces of fate or moral failure. A very direct line takes us from Oedipus to Macbeth to Willie Loman.

Classic tragedy has a parallel manifestation in the media's obsession with the never-ending collapse of the prominent, the powerful, and the rich into disgrace or misfortune. A front-page article in a recent issue of *The Dallas Morning News* tells of a man who was a senior adviser to the president while still in his twenties and a financial titan in his thirties. In his forties he was caught doctoring airline tickets and fined and sentenced to a federal penitentiary. In the process he lost a family, a career, and a reputation.[2] As William Inge once commented, "Nothing fails like success."

The public, incidentally, seems to take great pleasure in accounts of fame turned to infamy. The Germans have a word for it: *Schadenfreude*, literally "joy in harm," a perverse satisfaction over the downfall of the mighty.

The Bible and the Weakness of Strengths

Further to our point, a major theme of the Bible focuses upon the inordinate dangers of human strength. Indeed the Scriptures begin their account of human destiny on this note. We ask, did the prototypical humans, Adam and Eve, come to misery on account of their *weaknesses?* Far from it! Rather it was their *strengths* that brought them low—their proud defiance of God and the limitations he placed on them.

Further along in the Book of Genesis, we come upon the account of mortal men and women who, in a surge of arrogant power, built a tower by which they could invade the precincts of heaven and stand on a par with God. The exaltation of their strengths became their downfall.

Move along to Exodus, and there we encounter a monarch regarded as divine by his subjects. Only again it was not the weakness of Pharaoh that brought about his humiliation. Rather it was a heart hardened by insolent presumption of strengths.

Then, as Israel attained national status, we begin to read of how one king after another came to grief—again not through weakness as such but rather through a presumptuous reliance on military strength and political alliances.

Nor when, at last, Jesus of Nazareth came to live out his message did the murderous rejection of his ministry come about through human frailty. It came about primarily through human strengths, that is, a powerful coalition composed of the occupation forces of imperial Rome and the entrenched religious hierarchy of Jerusalem.

Jesus commented frequently upon the human tendency to become victimized by personal strengths. He declared that the endowment of riches was, in fact, an impoverishment, so far as the wealth of the Kingdom of God was concerned. And in one of his most stunning stories, he told of a prosperous farmer whose feelings of omnipotence overlooked the fundamental frailty of the human condition: mortality. As his wealth accumulated, the man decided to *raze* his old barns and *raise* new ones. Only in the midst of his vaulting ambition came God's voice: "You fool! This very night your life is being demanded of you. And the things you have prepared, whose will they be?"[3]

Strengths truly *do* serve as a primary source of weakness. Especially when employed in the cause of self-promotion will they, Jesus warned, function as the instrument of personal collapse. For this reason one must be wary of one's inherent gifts, as though handling dynamite. Especially explosive is the combination of known strengths and unknown weaknesses. Here

may be found one reason why personal strengths require conse-
cration—placement in the safekeeping of a greater-than-oneself.
Here also we find yet another reason why unrecognized weaknesses need raising to the level of analytical consciousness.

Success as the Greatest Hazard of All

To summarize, while personal weaknesses tend to remain concealed from conscious recognition, the opposite is true of
human strengths. We are quite aware of them, even though
they may not always be correctly assessed.

The principle that "your strengths are your weaknesses" suggests two paths. The first directs one toward a realistic appraisal
of strengths, however disillusioning the process may prove.
Those talents of which one may be assured should be accurately sized, so that they are proportional to their true value. At
the same time, one must come to terms with their relative danger under the formula: *the greater the strength, the greater the
danger.* And the greatest hazards of all can be expected if and
when that strength is crowned by success.

The second path returns in a circular fashion to the need for
discerning and acknowledging personal liabilities. Undetected
weaknesses tend to neutralize those strengths we do possess.
They can function as a powerful and poisonous alchemy that
can transform the gold—which is our talents—into base metal.

3

PRINCIPLE

Others Identify You and Deal with You On the Basis of Your Weaknesses, Not Your Strengths—I

Up to this point, our treatment of personal assets and liabilities has been more or less confined to the self in isolation. The first chapter focused broadly on human weaknesses, their inevitability, and their crucial influence upon life's destiny. We stated that, under the influence of powerful, instinctual drives, humans were programmed to conceal weaknesses from those around them.

We noted further that weaknesses were not only concealed from others but also routinely repressed from one's own conscious awareness as well. The result was a distortion of personality, augmented by the inability to define, much less pursue, a realistic set of life goals.

As a remedy, we suggested a program in which personal weaknesses would be given cognitive identification. The results would then be frankly admitted and openly confronted—to the self, to others, and to God. Such an approach, we declared, held the necessary power by which the self could become reoriented toward its authentic potential.

Chapter 2 shifted attention to personal *strengths*. We began with the postulate that, unlike weaknesses, personal strengths were well known to us. Far from being merely aware of our talents and assets, we humans tend to revel in them! As a result, we are tempted to overlook the liabilities that attach themselves parasitically to our strengths. We warned that the combination of evident strengths and unknown weaknesses could prove a disaster of nuclear proportions for any human being, largely because of the capacity of conspicuous strengths to conceal our most deadly vulnerabilities.

The insidious capacity of strengths to mask flaws can be illustrated by the experience of a friend from Maine who purchased a steel-hulled yacht for ocean cruising. The appearance of the vessel was impressive. Built in Holland, that mecca of seagoing ventures, the yacht's rakish lines indicated a modern, computer-enhanced design capable of handling the most demanding oceanic conditions. It carried the latest electronic navigational aids. Its cabins were luxuriously crafted. In short, the external image gave the impression of a vessel equal to the extended voyage planned by my friend. X-ray examination prior to embarkation, however, revealed structural corrosion within the hull so severe that the yacht was deemed essentially unseaworthy. Similarly, hidden weaknesses in human lives, when concealed by prominent strengths, can be all the more dangerous.

Implications for Relationships

Up to this point our examination of the role of personal strengths and weaknesses has been somewhat abstract. In general we have restricted our observations to the individual in isolation.

We now will begin to broaden the scope of our considerations by examining the practical impact of these principles upon our *relationships*. After all, the success and quality of life depend to a significant degree upon our ability to interact positively with others. "No man is an island," observed John Donne, the English poet and sometime Dean of St. Paul's. Life is dealt to us on a communal basis, one of its consequences being that the interior status of the self can generally be assessed by the quality of exterior relationships.

And so we are left to ask: What impact can increased awareness of personal weaknesses balanced by heightened *wariness* of personal strengths have upon our ability to communicate and deal effectively with others?

The answer could well be stated in the sort of terms ordinarily displayed on a theatre marquee: *Momentous! Phenomenal! Fantastic! Incredible! Exciting! Monumental!*

And just why do we feel justified in posting such a string of superlatives? The answer lies with our basic principle: to wit, *others identify us and deal with us on the basis of our weaknesses, not our strengths.* If this be true, and we shall so argue, then any increased awareness of personal weaknesses will bring about a commensurate heightening of our capacity to discern the approach *others take toward us.* This, in turn, will provide an immediate and dramatic improvement in the quality of inter-personal relationships.

Before proceeding, however, we must pause long enough to come to terms with the reasons why we are so intent on assuming that others have no real knowledge of our weaknesses, that we can readily conceal them to the point of invisibility, and that they are of little consequence in any event. What is it, moreover, that causes us to *insist* that others treat us according to the *strengths* we proudly set forth, even when those strengths are more fancied than real? One senses a powerful inner insurgency is at work. But what is it? Where are its origins to be found?

The Role of Competitiveness in Self-presentation

So that we might better grasp our innate tendency to display strengths and conceal weaknesses, so that we might better understand the influence thereof upon the give-and-take of ordinary human interchange, let us return to the issue of competitiveness in the human disposition. We shall concentrate our attention upon the crucial role competitive instincts play in the dynamics of engagement.

As noted in chapter 2, competition is a primary component of human behavior, a part of the "struggle for survival." To live is to compete, and the consequences thereof exert an enormous influence upon the structure and display of the human personality.

If there is any "story" inherent in the biological sciences it is of a pervasive competitive force that both animates and defines virtually all organic structures. The very composition of extant flora and fauna—their form, coloration, habits, chemical configurations—testify to the competitive demands that their place in the "chain of life" requires. Such competition not only demands a remorseless contention *between* the species but also a significant rivalry *within.* Who can fail to recognize that competition rules the den, the burrow, the nest—not to mention the home. Or consider the curious irony that even more highly-developed mammalian parents, which instinctively reproduce and nurture their offspring, seem ultimately doomed to become their children's competitors—and often deadly ones at that.

Humans share the same competitive urges found in the so-called lesser species. To exist presupposes a certain level of continuous strife with all other mortals, even those closest to us. Such instincts are programmed deeply, far below any capacity for cognitive control. Hidden in the inner recesses of the lower brain are powerful drives aimed at the procurement of territory, food, influence, power, and reproductive dominance. Indeed, it is within such a context that we might best comprehend the doctrine of "original sin," with its implication that the underlying evil from which no human can escape is the drive to subjugate all else to the self.

Despite its pervasiveness, competitiveness tends to be tempered by an opposite drive for bonding, also a requisite for survival. Even as we are driven to compete, we find ourselves necessarily *dependent* on one another. Fish must "school" for protection, various animals run in herds or packs or prides. Humans unite in families, societies, cultures, and nations. Thus the instinctual forces of competitiveness and bonding jostle vigorously within the human psyche, serving as primal ingredients in the drama of human experience. It has been aptly observed that people can neither live *with* nor *without* one another.

We would add here that the current emphasis upon "togetherness" tends to gloss over the furious fires of rivalry that burn just beneath the level of conscious awareness. Unabashed in the behavior of children, the competitive urge gradually becomes "civilized," revealing itself in such pastimes as gossip and small talk that essentially function as sublimated forms of competition. Yet closer to the basic instinct may be the athletic contests that so enthrall us and for which we pay our gladiators huge sums as they serve as surrogates in the ritual vanquishing of opponents.

Accordingly, even as we tout the power of love and extol the virtues of universal brotherhood and sisterhood, we find it all but impossible to escape the compulsion to deal with one another as adversaries. One's colleagues at the office, the Joneses next door, our relatives, spouses, offspring, even parents serve simultaneously as objects of affection—and foes. Freud's theory of Oedipal tension in the maturing process seizes upon this very point, with its recognition that the murderous albeit repressed rivalry of parent and offspring serves as a fundamental determinant of human behavior.

By its nature, the competitive instinct requires that each confrontation involves evaluation. The dog whose hair stands erect at the approach of an unrecognized and untested canine on the block epitomizes the competitive character of that species by bringing all senses to bear on this latest challenge: ears raised, eyes focused, nose collecting all sorts of data unavailable to human olfactory capacities, as the issue of dominance and submission is cast.

Just so, the human reaction to a stranger is the analytical "What do we have here?" The instinct is inborn and similar in function to that displayed throughout the natural order.

With humans, however, intellectual and critical faculties add to the process of evaluation as, along with the usual sensory perceptors, they are immediately trained on the newcomer in a manner that serves the survival mechanisms. Our very existence, in certain respects, depends upon our capacity to "make out" potential adversaries.

What so often escapes us, however, is the extent to which they too are evaluating us in turn. Ever quick to assess and judge the characteristics of others, in particular their vulnerabilities, we tend at the same time to remain oblivious to incoming perceptions, which are often far more accurate than we might prefer.

The Anatomy of Encounter

Ordinarily, the rite of encounter follows an instinctual pattern by which our strengths are made to confront the discerned weaknesses of others. At the same time—and the point is crucial—we attempt to *conceal* personal weaknesses and, further, *discount* what seems to us the potential strengths of the one being encountered.

Such an approach holds generally true for all organic entities, as may be illustrated by the often-observed phenomenon of animals making themselves appear larger and more formidable than they are.

In the case of human beings, however, a far broader range of response is available, with the result that an unchanging theme is given variations innumerable. For an uncomplicated personality, such as Stanley Kowalski in *A Streetcar Named Desire,* the equation—*personal strengths directed toward the other's weaknesses equal personal weaknesses concealed from the other's disparaged strengths*—is dealt with in a brutally direct manner. Such a person will brag or intimidate in the service of his competitive aims, even as he regards others with undisguised scorn for their feeble efforts to attempt the same.[1]

The great majority of humans, however, are not quite so ready-made. Those with passive-aggressive personalities, for instance, will handle strengths and weaknesses in self and others by methods far more Machiavellian. A typical strategy here is to display a competitively submissive exterior, while awaiting an opening for the thrust of a rapier. Such variations and their permutations abound, but the basic human approach is the same. In the encounter mode, a person will:

1. Display personal strengths, real or imagined;
2. Discern the weaknesses of the person being encountered and direct real or imagined strengths toward them;
3. Conceal personal weaknesses;
4. Discredit the apparent strengths of the one being encountered.

The process is instinctive, not calculated, and can be illustrated by virtually any situation in which one person confronts another for the first time. By way of illustration, let us imagine the nineteenth hole of a country club where a venerable member has just been introduced to the latest initiate. As jokes and small talk are exchanged over tonic, the elder subjects the younger to competitive assessment. Needless to say, he is being assessed in return, though likely unaware of it.

Were his inner emotions displayed like the "superscript" of an opera libretto over the proscenium, they might run as follows: "Where do they get these guys, anyway? This one probably sells mutual funds like all the rest. It's clear he bears watching. First thing you know he'll be after my place on the Greens Committee. Might even try to cozy up to my pals and make it harder than ever to scratch up a foursome."

In the thrust and parry that follows, the old member lays down a barrage of strengths, in particular his eminence as an elder statesman of the club. In ways both direct and indirect he tries to impress on the newcomer the fact that he knows who's who and what's what. These strengths are implicitly contrasted with the newcomer's weaknesses, which is to say his unfamiliarity with club procedures, rules, traditions, and pecking orders.

While directing his strengths toward the other's weaknesses, the older member brushes aside the novice's evident strengths, as, for example, the fact that the young man is successful in business, that he has a capable wife and achieving children, and, most importantly of all, that he plays to a five handicap.

Further, the elder is concerned to conceal his own vulnerabilities. Since, as we have already observed, personal weaknesses tend to be obscured from the self, he may be only dimly aware of what they are. For example, he may sense that he is not taken so seriously as he was in "the good old days." Occasionally, he feels oppressed by the suspicion that certain members seem to be avoiding him.

As he drones on with his list of personal credits, the old member remains oblivious to certain crucial liabilities, such as the fact that he has allowed himself to become overly garrulous and has turned into a bore. Besides, his play has slowed to a snail's pace, a trait made all the more annoying by his assumption that old members like himself no longer need observe the usual courtesies. Clearly were such weaknesses dealt with in the manner prescribed by this book—that is, were they both openly recognized and acknowledged—the outcome of this encounter might be more promising than its description would seem to suggest.

4

Others Identify You and Deal with You on the Basis of Your Weaknesses, Not Your Strengths—II

Because the role of weaknesses and strengths in the process of encounter is so crucial for productive, satisfying relationships, we will devote this chapter to a more detailed examination thereof, utilizing diagrams for visual reinforcement. Note that when we use the term *human-human encounter,* we are not necessarily referring to an initial meeting. We include all encounters, including those of the everyday variety with family members, neighbors, friends, and co-workers.

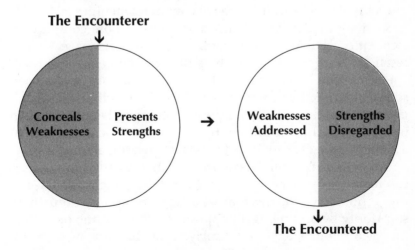

Human–Human Encounter (Figure 1)

Presentation of Strengths

Figure 1 indicates that when you find yourself in a typical encounter situation you put your "best foot forward." You do so primarily because of competitive instincts that prompt you to place the self in as invulnerable a position as possible. You may even prepare for competitive advantage, prior to actual engagement, by attiring yourself in a manner that suggests wealth, power, or influence, or by such cosmetic enhancement as will make you visually more beautiful, handsome, older, or younger.

Here, incidentally, may be found the power of "uniforms," with their suggestion of a collective competitive edge. Understood this way, the Sam Brown belt and the boots of police and military officers, not to mention the round collar and black suits of ecclesiastics, do not functionally differ from the leather attire of a Hell's Angel. All serve in part to establish competitive advantage in an encounter.

Sometimes a specified *absence* of uniform reflects a denial of competitive advantage, as when the Baptist preacher's plain necktie assures his congregation of the theoretical absence of spiritual hierarchy, with its accompanying conviction of the "priesthood of all believers."

Similarly, a tendency to underdress can also serve a semiotic purpose. In academic situations, for example, the wearing of rumpled tweed and unironed shirts can be a means of declaring one's intellectual elevation above common amenities.

Such adornment and their accompanying pose comprise an element of what Tournier describes as one's "personage." Let us recall yet once more that if the authentic self consists of one's "person," with its intermingled strengths and frailties, the "personage," by contrast, serves as the idealized self-image that is projected upon others for purposes of competitive edge. By various means, subtle or brazen, the personage functions as a self-aggrandizing facade intended to achieve relational purchase.

Displays of the personage are as varied as the human race can make them. Some are given spectacular presentation, seemingly intended, like the roar of a tiger, to attain competitive superiority by unhinging all opposition. At times the projected, idealized self-image will be displayed fraudulently, as in criminal acts of impersonation when, without credentials, one feigns status as a physician, a military figure, or a police officer. In most cases, however, human efforts at pretense are more in the nature of a game of upmanship and often performed so badly as to arouse amusement or scorn in others.

A merry example may be found in Oliver Goldsmith's charming novel *The Vicar of Wakefield,* where Dr. Primrose, the high-minded but bumbling protagonist of the story, succumbs to the temptation of flattering image-projection by having his family painted in the heroic manner peculiar to his time—the eighteenth century. A traveling artist is hired and subsequently instructed to depict the vicar's wife as Venus, with her two youngest as Cupids. The vicar himself is to be shown resplendent in clerical attire presenting to his Venus a vanity volume from his pen on an obscure religious controversy. He is flanked by a daughter represented as an Amazon, while yet another daughter is portrayed as a shepherdess "with as many sheep as the painter could put in for nothing." As the work evolves, the local squire becomes so impressed that he insists on being added to the ensemble as Alexander the Great. A difficulty arises, however, when it is found that the finished canvas is much too large for the rectory walls and must suffer the consequent indignity of being cut into pieces in order to be removed through the kitchen door.

The Concealment of Weaknesses

Even as strengths are presented in an encounter, Figure 1 indicates that weaknesses are kept out of sight. The immediate reason for concealment is their adverse effect on the competitive edge. A substrata of causative factors will be involved, such as the fear that any revelation of personal frailties will automatically rule one out of competition by reason of self-evident inferiority.

It is to this endemic human anxiety that Karen Horney alludes in her epic study *The Neurotic Personality of Our Time*, suggesting that "the neurotic fear of disapproval" constitutes one of the most powerful factors in human interaction.[1] Anyone afflicted by a neurosis, however inconsequential—and this would include the vast majority of the human race—are made anxious, she states, by the assumption that others will reject them if they are discovered to be nothing more than the frail, fallible mortals they are. It is such insecurity, Horney suggests, that lies at the foundation of garden variety neuroses. "Nearly every neurotic, even though he appear on surface observation to be entirely certain of himself and indifferent to the opinion of others, is excessively afraid of or hypersensitive to being disapproved of, criticized, accused, found out," she observes.[2]

Perceived Weaknesses Addressed

The diagram further shows that, in any confrontation, the encounterer not only displays strengths while concealing weaknesses but also directs those strengths toward the presumed weaknesses of the other. Though appearing friendly and admiring, the encounterer attempts to isolate the other's vulnerabilities and ordinarily does so with considerable acumen. What are the faults, blemishes, handicaps, disorders, and other liabilities in this person that can provide me with competitive advantage?

This process of balancing an inflated self-image with a deflated appraisal of the encountered might be likened to the difference between the heroic portraiture lampooned in *The Vicar of Wakefield* and the artistic genre known as caricature. Functionally, the caricature relies for its effectiveness upon the discernment of imperfections, along with their magnification. The caricaturist fashions the long chin of his study into a promontory, the pronounced brow into a precipice, spectacles into goggles, the ski-slope nose into a ski jump.

What we suggest is that the more anxious or inferior one may feel in an encounter situation, the more one will tend to regard the self as a Venus or Alexander the Great. Simultaneously, the person being encountered will have minor imperfections expanded into grotesque proportions and often be dismissed as little more than a freak.

Many, reading these words, will deny that they so react. But the pervasiveness of the tendency is surely exhibited in the commonplace behavior of children, who possess an instinctive capacity to discern flaws in others and to overreact to them. Parents are at first amused, then horrified by the cruel candor of their offspring until there comes a point when there is no option beyond intensive instructions in the essentials of polite behavior. Parents will accordingly begin to issue stern warnings about such practices as staring, tittering, whispering, and other evidences of ridicule directed toward the oddities of others.

Children may display a surface shyness, but at deeper levels they are disposed to be contemptuous of others, even as they regard themselves the measure of all things, exhibiting scant awareness of their own limitations. An unabashed confidence in their own presumed superiority, together with a natural talent for bullying and bragging, accounts in some measure for those perennial discussions among children that seldom stray from an obsessive concern to know who or what is to be despised and why. Such fixation will be disguised in the maturing process, but hardly forsaken.

Evident Strengths Disregarded

Finally, the diagram suggests that the instinctual urge to identify and exploit the weaknesses of persons being encountered is accompanied by a tendency to minimize evident strengths. Characteristically one will employ here that qualifier-of-preference *but.* "She may be beautiful, but ———— " "He may seem successful, but ———— "

Disparagement is a universal tendency. The urge to cut others "to size" must only be regarded as inescapable since the failure to do so seems a concession of competitive superiority without challenge.

Consider, for example, the common practice of peppering compliments with invidious provisos. A person being congratulated for some level of success will frequently find himself the object of gratuitous "put-downs" as well. The manner of delivery may *seem* cordial but be full of daggers nonetheless. In the context of our discussion, the reason for such ambiguity is not difficult to identify. It comes simply of that inborn human competitiveness that refuses unalloyed deference. Who has not experienced the thorns lurking in presumably genial compliments and left to salt the resulting wounds with Hamlet's observation that "one may smile and smile and be a villain"?

The tendency to present one's strengths and conceal weaknesses, while discerning weaknesses and disregarding the strengths of others, will have become a fully-developed form of competitive behavior by early childhood. Kept within appropriate bounds—which is to say tempered by such virtues as graciousness, self-deprecation, and forbearance as instilled by parents, peers, teachers, and church—the tendency can serve as a healthy component of survival instincts. When misapplied, however, as when a person develops an unrealistically grandiose self-image combined with an obsessional hypercriticism of others, one may teeter toward paranoid psychosis on the one hand or personality disorders on the other.

Recognizing the tendency in both self and others indicates the importance of a methodical investigation of personal weaknesses. It also provides a poignant reminder of the general cussedness of the human race, with its universal bent for grabbing and squabbling, strutting and posing, and its seemingly uncontrollable urge to criticize the undefended and the absent in a negative, mean-spirited manner. Indeed it may well be here, in the realm of competitive evaluation, that one finds the roots of racial and other forms of discrimination. To recognize as much not only helps account for the unrelenting tenacity of such behaviors but also indicates the glimmer of a solution.

For some reason, the competitive urge is especially evident when religion is involved, despite all claims to the contrary. Religious elitism will always remain a hardy weed, as one body of conviction casts its presumed spiritual superiority against the presumed religious inadequacies of others.

Symptomatic of religious competitiveness is a preoccupation over who is "in" and who is "out." The game is played in our day with equal fervor by liberals and conservatives, both of whom promote rigorous orthodoxies and maintain them by an elaborate set of passwords that enables constituents to identify their own kind, even as they despise others. Jesus condemned such tendencies for their withering effect upon the humble seeker of truth: "Woe to you, scribes, pharisees—hypocrites! It is not enough that you yourselves refuse to enter the Kingdom; but you keep out those who would!"[3]

Beyond the Search for Admiration

A recognition of one's relentlessly competitive nature frees us from some of its more pernicious consequences, such as futile efforts at creating an impression. By understanding that as we deal with others, so, in turn, will we be dealt with, we will help neutralize the misdirected energy that maintains those grandiose self-projections by which we deceive ourselves. Not only are others able to detect our weaknesses with an ability that outpaces our own but also they appropriately scorn the masks by which we attempt to dissemble them. Even if one is sufficiently clever to "one-up" all others for the moment, the long-term response will not be admiration but rather gathering resentment accompanied by an intensified search for vulnerabilities—probing for flaws in both performer and performance. Thus one can be assured that even if concealing weaknesses behind a facade may succeed for a time, the stratagem will ultimately fail as observers become suspicious, disillusioned, impatient, and, ultimately, contemptuous and indifferent.

Recognizing that others can both discern our weaknesses and deal with us accordingly will begin a process of release from that self-created prison called the personage. Gradually we find ourselves delivered of the temptation to brag or pose; to act coy, cute, or sophisticated; to match talents, experiences, connections, abilities, or possessions; to play such games as "Who Do You Know?," "Where Have You Been?," "What Have You Seen?," "What Have You Read?"; and all the other sorts of useless ego-preening tricks we employ and for the reinforcement of which we all too often turn to alcohol and drugs. Neither need we bother ourselves with self-pitying rage directed toward others who do not treat us according to our pretensions. Delivered from unproductive attempts to maneuver or dazzle, we can become free to deal with others at the level of empathy and objectivity, the only basis upon which sound human interaction can be assured.

The effects of a heightened awareness of personal weakness can become manifest even under the most mundane circumstances. An automobile showroom will serve as a convenient example. Consider two scenarios. In the first, you enter and pass yourself off as a sophisticated, intelligent, socially-prominent, and successful man (or woman)-about-town. In other words, you display that mixture of genuine strengths and contrived strengths that constitute your personage. Your purpose, even if you are not consciously aware of it, is to gain competitive advantage.

Since the salesman, by nature of his profession, is adept at discerning the true status of potential buyers, he will quickly make a few shrewd guesses about the vulnerabilities that lie behind your projected strengths. With this knowledge, he begins to use your self-projections to his own advantage, exploiting the very weaknesses that you presume to hide. You, in turn, assume he is dealing with you on the basis of your displayed strengths, making you all the more susceptible to his manipulation. In the meantime, straightforward communication has become the first victim of this encounter.

In the alternative scenario, you enter the showroom not only aware of your weaknesses but content for them to be known. You acknowledge that automobiles interact with your vanity, that you tend to buy over budget, and that your credit can be compared to a rubber band stretched to its limit. Nevertheless, you are interested in at least seeing what the dealer has to offer. The salesman may wish, under the circumstances, that he was dealing with an idealized self-image but must be content with unabashed self-disclosure. At least, both parties will benefit from a realistic set of transactions.

In short, *a comprehensive understanding of personal weaknesses, together with the willingness to make them known, will bring almost instantaneous improvement in relationships of all kinds.* The precept cannot be gainsaid. Others *will* identify you and deal with you on the basis of your weaknesses, not your strengths. To know this, principle and practicalities alike, will yield incomparable treasures, not least an increased capacity to deal positively and productively with others.

Others Know Us Better than We Know Ourselves

Now we are left to consider the crowning irony of all: namely that others, even slight acquaintances, tend to know us better than we know ourselves. Nietzsche's trenchant insight could not be more accurate: "Everyone is furthest from himself."[4] Obviously he does not refer here to the trivia of life, such as shoe size or street number. Rather he speaks of the total picture.

Individually we may hold the facts and figures that detail our existence—everything from our innermost thoughts to the hour and minute of our birth. But like the trees of a forest, an underbrush of details often obscures the panorama. Clemenceau's observation of his political rival, Raymond Poincaré, is one that could be readily applied to the understanding we all have of ourselves: "He knows everything, but understands nothing."

Can it be that the store clerk who rings up your charge of $7.31 of groceries will be granted, in those few moments, a far more balanced impression of the real you than anything you yourself possess? To the extent that you remain unaware of the nature and extent of your weaknesses it will be so.

Then what better pathway to positive dealings with those whose lives impinge on ours than a comprehensive inventory of personal weaknesses? What better method for beginning a sensible and relaxed approach to all encounters? Relationships, after all, must be formed by the warp of curiosity and the woof of self-disclosure, flaws included. Unless these threads can become reliably interwoven, no fabric can be hoped for.

Robert Burns's well-worn words in "To a Louse" come to mind:

> *O wad some Power the giftie gie us*
> *To see oursels as ithers see us!*

Nor dare we forget his conclusion of the matter:

> *It wad frae monie a blunder free us,*
> *An' foolish notion. . . .*

5

God Knows Us and Deals with Us on the Basis of Our Weaknesses, Not Our Strengths—I

Lord Melbourne, who as prime minister and principle adviser to Queen Victoria stood at the apex of British imperial power 150 years ago, made the following observation: "Neither man nor woman can be worth anything until they have discovered that they are fools. This is the first step towards becoming either estimable or agreeable; and until it be taken there is no hope."

Melbourne's words aptly describe our progress to date, which may be summarized as follows:

1. The recognition and admission of personal weaknesses show the way forward;
2. Personal strengths may be the greatest hazards we face;
3. We might just as well accept 1 and 2 because others identify and deal with us primarily on the basis of our weaknesses anyway.

As we approach a practical method for uncovering those weaknesses, which lie within the fogs of self-deception, as we anticipate the strengths that can become unleashed through perception of those weaknesses, there remains one area where the principle, your weaknesses are your strengths, requires examination. Unquestionably, it is the most fascinating consideration of all, inasmuch as it lies so close to the central question of life's meaning. In short, we turn now to the cosmic aspects of this principle: *God too both knows us and deals with us on the basis of our weaknesses, not our strengths.* Such an assertion carries with it the most pressing of all reasons for comprehending personal frailty and fault; namely, that such awareness provides a passage to the very foundations of our existence.

In order to fathom the nature of this principle, it will be necessary to discuss two corresponding issues: first, what we might describe as the "natural" or inborn attitude of human beings toward deity; and, second, what many believe to be the "revealed" attitude of God toward us.

At this point I might recommend that the dedicated secularist leap over the intervening pages to chapter 7, inasmuch as my approach will now make a decidedly orthodox Christian turn. It seems only right that I further run up my colors as an Anglican in the Model-T mode, whose understanding of the relationship of the human to the divine has its source in that theological trinity composed of Saint Paul, Saint Augustine, and John Calvin, with their collective affirmation that the only means by which one can approach the realm of the Divine is through awareness and admission of personal weakness. The term that describes this process is *confession.*

Acknowledgment of Weaknesses: A Prerequisite to Knowledge of God

The basic premise of Pauline-Augustinian-Calvinistic thought rests firmly on the principle that God interacts with us *only* on the basis of an expressed, mutually acknowledged, and realistic assessment of our seriously weakened condition as mortal beings.

This is so primarily because such is the truth of the human situation. Since God is Truth, he does not deal falsely with anything or anyone. God does not traffic in such fantasies as the notion that humans are lesser gods or are possessed of unlimited potentialities. God *starts* with the fact of human weaknesses. Conseqently, the person who neither perceives nor acknowledges weaknesses simply lacks the necessary wherewithal by which any knowledge of or association with God can be realized.

To put the matter conversely, no greater barrier to the realm of the Eternal can exist than reliance upon personal strengths, especially when those strengths are accompanied by, as is ordinarily the case, a presumptuous denial of personal weaknesses.

Admission of fault and frailty provides the only path to the God—or, more accurately, his to us. The loving Deity of the Bible deals with us only on the basis of a frank acknowledgment of our fatally flawed condition because, once again, such is the truth of things, and God deals with us truly.

A hearty appreciation of this principle is what lies behind the apostle Paul's declaration of the fundamental paradox of the Christian religion: "When I am weak, then am I strong."[1] It was his way of stating that the confession, repentance, acceptance-of-grace axis provides sole entry to divine empowerment.

What makes this basic Christian presupposition all the more astonishing is the corresponding belief that God approaches the realities of the human condition not from the vectors of power but rather from what can only be interpreted as an abject display of divine weakness—a perception that distinguishes the Christian religion from all others. As we shall attempt to point out in chapter 6, even as God rejects human strength by his righteous adherence to truth, so he solicits our devotion by a divine humility that renders him vulnerable to false and presumptuous human strengths, yes, even a murderous effort to remove him from the commonwealth of humanity altogether.

Only through the recognition and acknowledgment of personal deficiency are humans able to discern the paradox that God's weaknesses provide the enablements for their strengths. This profound yet accessible paradox not only holds the power of reconciliation for the fragmented personality, not only heals disrupted external relationships but also is able to bond the self to the very source of Reality. Here the interweavings of our governing principle—your weaknesses are your strengths—can be apprehended as a single seamless garment. The truth applies, as it were, "every which way"—inwardly, outwardly, upwardly. The key to the fulfillment of the self—be that fulfillment a sense of inner integration, a capacity for positive relationships, or a faith-bond with God—lies with personal weaknesses discerned, acknowledged, repented for.

God as Adversary

What is so very fascinating here is the extent to which our ordinary orientation toward God is precisely opposite that required for a faith-bond. Opinion polls suggest that people are by nature religious. In truth, humans are born regarding God as an alien possibility, and so they will remain without that dramatic reversal of attitude called repentance.

We do not speak here of conventional religiosity. Of that there is no shortage. The religious sentimentality associated with, for example, the greeting card industry or country western lyrics infers a sort of universal piety. But the assumptions could hardly be more wide off the mark. Anyone who believes that human beings are automatically religious, that by nature they acknowledge a Supreme Being and do so with unbounded devotion, has simply not contemplated the realities of the human condition.

While it may be argued that one is born with an inchoate sense of transcendence, as Paul allows in the first chapter of Romans, such intimations do not necessarily translate into a coherent belief system, much less a universal religious devotion. Without doubt, Paul goes on to make clear that *rejection* of sovereign transcendence is the customary human attitude.

Why is this so? The answer once again lies with competitiveness—the determination to exalt the self at the expense of all others, God included. Autonomy remains the first item on the human agenda. Such autonomy translates sooner or later into rebellion directed against all constitutive powers, both earthly and heavenly. Parents, peers, society, and God—all become targets of the individual's struggle for self-assertion. The angry cry of the baby provides an audible if nonverbal manifestation of the human inclination to order up the universe to one's tastes. It is at such primal levels that we discover the truth about our natural religious aptitude—certainly not at the level of "Praying Hands."

Indifference as an Adversarial Pose

Rebellion against one's Creator only rarely takes the form of explicit rejection. More often than not its expression is disdain, which is to say the sort of indifference we associate with the callow youth who remains resolutely seated, hat on head, as the flag is trooped by. What must be recognized of religious apathy is the fact that a contemptuous dismissal of religion's claims, even if expressed by a yawn, is merely the flip of pride's coin. One's sense of occupying the center of the universe is what renders the eternal moot.

The resulting arrogance serves as the engine that compels us to make God a topic of discussion, rather than a focus of worship. Those notorious "bull sessions" on religion, so popular among college students, tend to have less to do with Almighty God than the Almighty Self, especially when oiled by alcohol. While still a youngster, Thérèse of Lisieux was able to discern the smug religion-of-self that attended supposedly earnest conversations about God. Her keen insight brought her to the conclusion that people would do far better attempting to talk to rather than about him.[2]

This is not to say that feelings of ultimate dependency will never occur. Even those described by Friedrich Schleiermacher as the "cultured despisers of religion" will have an occasional mystical experience of "the starry sky above . . . the moral law within" or a fleeting encounter with what Rudolf Otto characterizes as the "wholly other."[3] But fitful episodes of this nature will have little impact upon the normal tendency to regard God as a negligible, if not nagging, factor in the effort at sole self-possession. One is reminded of Isak Dinesen's definition of God as "He who says No."

We therefore dismiss any suggestion of inborn religiosity. God exists primarily in the popular mind precisely as portrayed in the opening pages of the Bible. In its broadest dimensions, the story of Adam and Eve is an account of a pervasive human contempt for the sovereignty of God, together with an equally pervasive unwillingness to acknowledge personal weaknesses. Two prototypical humans, a man and a woman, surface to self-conscious existence in a bountiful Eden under the mysterious benevolence of their Creator. It is not long, however, before they are tempted to believe that they can grasp for themselves what has been given on condition of obedience to those universal laws that guarantee their good. Convinced as they are of being able to distinguish good from evil as fully and capably as God, the two defy the divine decrees in the tragic assumption that they can serve themselves better than their Maker. All their rebellion brings, however, is the severing of ties with the very Source of life.

Proud, posturing power; arrogant denial of weakness—these are the applications of human strengths that form an impenetrable barrier against God. As illustrated in Figure 2, the stance tracks the human-divine encounter precisely.

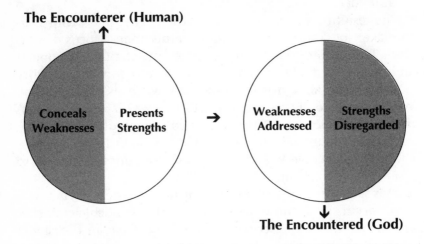

The Encounterer (Human)

| Conceals Weaknesses | Presents Strengths | → | Weaknesses Addressed | Strengths Disregarded |

The Encountered (God)

Human–Divine Encounter (Figure 2)

Encounterer (Human) Presents Strengths

The manner in which humans confront the ultimates of life is a subject that could easily fill volumes inasmuch as it is the stuff of art, philosophy, and religion. Pursuing the issue raised in the previous section, we now ask: What *is* the typical attitude of humans toward the "beyond?" How best to describe raw human nature in its orientation toward that for which we use the term *God?*

Figure 2 initially suggests an inherent human tendency to confront the supernatural, however perceived, from the stance of personal strengths. The posture mirrors that of the self toward fellow human beings. The characteristic attitude toward the divine might thus be illustrated by the unjust judge in Jesus' humorous parable who, assured of his privileged status, fears "neither God nor man." Thus, far from being viewed in a spirit of awe, "God" is regarded as but one more exterior factor to the self that needs to be reckoned with much in the same manner as any potential human infringement upon individual "territory."[4]

Such an assessment of the human stance, vis-à-vis God, runs counter to the popular assumption that people generally revere deity. Even under conditions where an excess of piety seems to exist, as in the so-called Bible Belt, one is nevertheless bound to inquire what sort of God serves as the object of that presumed universal reverence or how that reverence actually manifests itself. For example, were belief in a God of moral judgment widespread, would we not find ourselves in a far less violent and greed-stricken world than is presently the case?

Demonstrably, the greater portion of those who say they defer to a Supreme Being do not seem to attach much moral consequence to their belief, as is indicated by a world awash in substance abuse, racism, promiscuity, exploitation, predatory behavior, and so forth. "In God We Trust" may be printed on our currency, but that same currency, widely dispersed among the world's population, finds itself being used not in the service of that deity but more commonly in the perpetration of international crime.

A God to Be Feared or the Man Upstairs?

Polls continue to proclaim that a high percentage of Americans believe in a deity of some sort. Most acknowledge him, or "it," or even "she" as a supernatural dispenser of favors that can be cajoled or cozened from time to time, especially if one happens to find oneself cowering in one of the foxholes of life.

Still, we are left to ask how many actually live in the "fear of the Lord," which is to say mindful that a sovereign judgment stands over the most minute determinations of the will. The Bible repeatedly affirms its basic credo that "the fear of the Lord is the beginning of wisdom." Stating the matter conversely gives a keener edge: there can be no greater folly than a condescending or nonchalant attitude toward the divine. One's God can be nothing if not a God to evoke terror.

Nevertheless, we are left with the melancholy likelihood that only those trained to fear God will be inclined to do so. The remainder, in particular those who, as children, were permitted by liberalized parents to "choose for themselves" a congenial religious orientation, seem doomed to lapse into a wary indifference toward anything above or beyond themselves. Either that or they will surrender to cult fanaticism, which is but another form of self-exaltation.

Are earnest, pious parents required, then, it may be wondered, for the inner conviction that one's Creator is a present and consequential Being not to be trifled with? So it would appear. In other words, inbred attitudes about God seem necessary if religion is to become a serious factor in one's life.

Here may be found one reason why liberal Christianity so often fails to be perpetuated down through the generations. Unable to train children with more than a casual take-it-or-leave-it approach toward religion, parents bequeath little more than a God of options that can be pursued in more or less the same desultory manner as any other beautiful but nonessential ideal. Religion thus conveyed may come to be regarded as a reinforcement of social or patriotic values, but is seldom considered for its own sake. A not-to-be-taken-seriously God thus turns into "the man upstairs," a superannuated bumbler aptly played by George Burns, a deity fabricated by humans in the interests of profit.

Such condescension may be compared with a no-nonsense religion such as Islam, which succeeds in part because it displaces natural attitudes of autonomous selfhood with a ruthlessly efficient conditioning in "submission" to Allah that becomes relentlessly transmitted from generation to generation.[5]

Thus, we conclude that the attitude toward Transcendence that is described in Scriptures as the "fear of the Lord" is hardly natural and, what's more, never has been. By nature we are disposed to regard all outside the self from a posture of personal strengths, God included.

Encounterer (Human) Conceals Weaknesses

The inherent tendency of humans to conceal weakness in their encounter with the divine is reflected in the story of Adam and Eve's clothing themselves after the Fall. This act is often regarded as part of the divine punishment. But should it not also be considered as an aspect of the primary rebellion? Nakedness must be concealed because it reveals all too clearly humanity's kinship with the lesser animals. Humans find it difficult to believe that they are not gods; that, instead, they are animals in every respect save a spiritual capacity for self-transcendence conferred by a power other than themselves.

Humans thus conceal their inherent weaknesses in the face of the eternal through an effort to appear as gods, not the creatures they are, by adorning those areas of the body that house the apparatus of perception and will. Hair is shorn. Beard removed. Eyes and eyebrows are enhanced. The mouth is prominently displayed.

Concurrently, the organs of reproduction and elimination are concealed, indicative of that mortal hubris that desires to conceal animality, even while displaying the self as standing at least on an equal footing with God.

Research by archaeologists and anthropologists indicates that humans have tended to attire themselves in the manner of the gods from earliest times. From a historical perspective, it could be held that priestly and royal garments serve little purpose. Robes and vestments hide one's "sweating self and worse" even though they succeed only to a limited degree. To the guileless they will always remain the "emperor's clothes" of Hans Christian Andersen's tale because of their transparent inability to conceal such inherent frailties as mortality, self-absorption, guilt, greed, and ignorance.

The Weaknesses of the Encountered (God) Are Addressed

Figure 2 further indicates that humans characteristically direct their strengths toward the presumed weaknesses of God. Again, the attitude is innate. The human personality is so arranged that nothing in this world or beyond is allowed parity with those wants and needs that constitute its self-assertion—not even God. God may be permitted a contributing role, as may be observed among televangelists and others who traffic in that lucrative business that compounds egoism and credulity. Nevertheless, despite fervid adulation of the divine by the hucksters of religion, one cannot escape the suspicion that what truly occupies stage center is not so much deity as ego. God's status is merely complimentary *and* complementary. The sun turns out to be oneself. Around that heliocenter all else revolves, God included, as satellites held in the self's field of gravity. Albert Camus's words in *The Fall* express the matter aptly: "I, I, I is the refrain of my whole life."[6]

From the promontory of self-assertion, one has little difficulty pointing out the weaknesses of God. Two may be said to stand out: 1) the seeming inability of deity to authenticate itself and 2) theodicy.

Nonverification as a Divine Weakness

The lack of a coherent proof system for God's existence is well established. The Scottish philosopher David Hume concluded that there were no rational means by which a case for deity could be made. Job discovered as much. Even the Psalmist cried for God to come and "show thyself," as though despairingly aware that the heavens would remain adamantly shut notwithstanding.[7]

Any purported crack in the impenetrable canopy will invariably draw hordes of the credulous. But "proof" remains elusive, leaving cynicism in its wake. Visions of the Virgin, weeping statues, televangelist healings, ghostsightings, or messages from "the other side" reported by mediums continue to provide a source of income for those clever and unscrupulous enough to capitalize on human longing for supernatural verification. As H. L. Mencken pointed out, no one ever got poor by overestimating the religious credulity of the American public.

For the majority, however, God's far more evident absence will remain an indication of divine weakness, which is to say his seeming incapacity to enter the scene and clear up the confusion. Worse, for some, is the possibility that the lack of a convincing demonstration of divine reality adds up to cold, cosmic indifference. Here the presumed divine weakness is given a sinister spin. A character in John Fowles's novel *The Collector* says: "I still believe in a God. But he's so remote, so cold, so mathematical. I see that we have to live as if there is no God. Prayer and worship and singing hymns—all silly and useless."[8]

Both interpretations are commonly held. Not that counterarguments are unavailable, however. Some suggest that God's hiddenness, far from being a weakness, serves as a functional necessity for a deity that would solicit fellowship from its spiritual kin on the basis of unhindered choice. A love relationship requires conditions of absolute freedom—a capacity to give or withhold unfettered by coercion. Thus a divine wooer, plaintive and uncertain, is required if human beings are to respond freely. In his recent autobiography, *Self-Consciousness: Memoirs*, John Updike makes this very point: "The sensation of (God's) silence cannot be helped: a loud and evident God would be a bully, an insecure tyrant, an all-crushing datum instead of, as He is, a bottomless encouragement to our faltering and frightened being."[9]

Updike's argument echoes that of contemporary philosopher Alasdair MacIntyre: "If the existence of God were demonstrable we should be as bereft of the possibility of making a free decision to love God as we should be if every utterance of doubt or unbelief was answered by thunderbolts from heaven."[10]

Samuel Terrien broadens the matter in his fascinating study, *The Elusive Presence*.[11] He observes that Scriptures, far from suffering embarrassment at the lack of substantive evidence for God's existence, accept it enthusiastically as a crucial element in the divine plan. Terrien prefaces his book with a quotation from Pascal: "A religion which does not affirm that God is hidden is not true. *Vere, tu es Deus absconditus.*"

Existence of Evil as Indicative of Divine Weakness

A second, and more poignant allegation of God's weakness, known as *theodicy*, asks how an omniscient, benevolent God can permit evil. The classic disclaimer states that innocent suffering proves either divine weakness or divine indifference, leaving one with the choice between a God who is good but not all-powerful and one who is all-powerful but not good.

Dostoyevsky poses the Job-like challenge in *The Brothers Karamazov*. Ivan addresses Alyosha: "Tell me yourself, I challenge you—answer. Imagine that you are creating a fabric of human destiny with the object of making men happy in the end, giving them peace and rest at last, but that it was essential and inevitable to torture to death only one tiny creature—that baby beating its breast with its fist, for instance—and to found that edifice on its unavenged tears, would you consent to be the architect on those conditions?'"[12]

Encountered's (God's) Strengths Are Disregarded

The natural tendency to disregard the strengths of God has been touched on so often in this chapter and elsewhere that elaboration would be merely redundant. We might, however, consider one prevalent indication of the universality of this trait: namely, the common practice of profanity.

Profanity is often regarded as a violation of the Third Commandment, "Thou shalt not take the name of the Lord thy God in vain." The interpretation is dubious. The commandment, in fact, refers to the breaking of one's promise, especially when that vow has been given sacred reinforcement by invoking the presence of God. Thus to swear to something in his name, then renege, is truly to take God's name for naught.

Rather, profanity may find its niche under the summary commandment that urges us to love (that is, to "care for" or "revere") the Lord our God with all our heart, soul, and might.[13] As the fulcrum of God's identity, the divine name is to be cared for and hallowed, as the Lord's Prayer entreats, not used as an expression of rage or frustration. The ancient Jewish custom of refraining from uttering aloud the sacred Name expressed by the mysterious tetragrammaton *JHWH*—no, not even in liturgical worship—served as an acknowledgment of a godly strength that extended beyond all apparent weakness. The hallowing of the divine Name thus became a reminder of the fathomless abyss of divine strengths that can all too easily be overlooked by humans in their insolent self-idolatry.

Profanity takes us in the opposite direction. As presently chorused in plays, movies, and everyday conversation, the expletive use of the Name vitiates both the strengths and the gracious weaknesses of God through a process of trivialization.

6

PRINCIPLE

God Knows Us and Deals with Us on the Basis of Our Weaknesses, Not Our Strengths—II

In order to complete our understanding of the principle that "God knows us and deals with us on the basis of our weaknesses, not our strengths," we must also raise the question of how God approaches us. What happens when God becomes the encounterer and we the encountered?

The question is absorbing for a number of reasons, beginning with the admission that we have no way of providing a verifiable answer. The fact remains that we cannot be certain there is a God. Further, if God does exist, what indication have

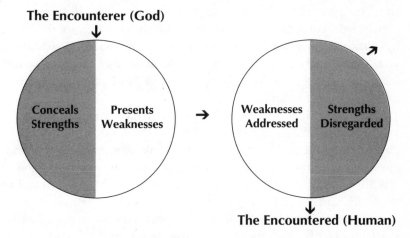

Divine–Human Encounter (Figure 3)

we that such a deity has any dealings with, indeed cognizance, of the human situation? Taking up Milton's quest of justifying the ways of God to man, we will never get beyond that interpretation of hints and events that is called "faith." Faith is always interpretation in any event, never credulity.

Thus, if we are going to reverse our diagram and speak for the far side of the equation, we have no option but to enlist an "authority" that can provide a "revelation" of those concerns of which we know little to nothing. Assuming, then, that such an authority can be found in what we will call the "mind of the Bible," what can be stated on the matter?

Encounterer (God) Presents Weaknesses

Curiously, it is not divine power that characterizes the Bible's record of God's encounter with humanity so much as the divine *vulnerability*. Hebrew thought brushes aside Greek philosophical assertions of the remoteness and impassibility of the deity and presents a God who arbitrarily changes his mind; acts out of anger, jealousy, and indignation; laughs; expresses regret; and behaves like a foolish, indulgent father with his disobedient children, even while seemingly unable to come to terms with those deep, malevolent forces that make his precepts virtually unattainable in the first place.

The biblical God indeed appears so changeable, so arbitrary that the apostle Paul seems obliged to defend the divine sovereignty by declaring that God deliberately chooses weakness as his modus operandi.[1] That this may be necessary is discussed later. But, for the moment, let us acknowledge that Scriptures leave anything but the impression of a God of unambiguous power and perfection.

The divine weakness extends itself in a variety of curious ways, as, for example, the apparent intent of the God of Scriptures to choose less-than-admirable vessels as his agents in this world. Not the illustrious, but the marginal are summoned to the divine mission. Abraham and Sarah begin the lineage of revelation, but they are hardly the stuff of epics; neither do they come across as moral paragons. Isaac, their son, is portrayed as a dupe, while grandson Jacob steals his claim to the divine mission and, in various other ways, proves himself a rogue and a scoundrel.

Moses appears somewhat later and while popular tradition portrays him as a folk hero, a careful reading of Exodus reveals an unstable personality. The judges and kings who thereafter emerge to lead the holy nation have a way of emanating from dubious backgrounds, and their foibles are recorded with relish. Samson, for example, is depicted as being rather on the order of a football star who has played without his helmet once too often. Eli is revealed as a foolish, overindulgent parent. The eventually mad king Saul seems to have been selected more on the basis of height than heredity, while David's origins are those of a minor son without so much as a claim on the family inheritance. Even the prophets who served as God's oracles are, by ordinary standards, a questionable lot. Amos could be described as an unemployed nurseryman with a grudge, Hosea a willing cuckold, Elijah a welter of manic-depressive tendencies, Elisha a man of mental instability. Indeed the prophetic ministry as a whole, and in particular the wandering "school" of prophets (*n'bim*), seems more a traveling sideshow of freaks than emissaries of the most high God.

Incarnation as Supreme Divine Weakness

The New Testament carries the theme of the divine weakness to its apogee, depicting God's seemingly desperate desire to secure human acceptance as a process of abject abandonment of omnipotence. He arrives on the scene through the pregnancy of an unwed teenager. Reared in an obscure backwater, the divine-become-human moves onto the scene well past his prime, only to be regarded as a neurotic, inebriate, maverick, and blasphemer. Accordingly, he finds himself reviled, mocked, rejected, and ultimately executed under conditions of extreme public humiliation.

It is such a shocking display of divine meekness and weakness that Paul, with his keen logic, is finally compelled to describe it as the "folly" of the cross. Such a "folly," he admits, will inevitably be dismissed by the rational Greek intellect as silly, even while being repudiated by the theologically-oriented Jew as an unimaginably offensive sacrilege. Yet, Paul asserts that this unlikely manifestation of divine weakness is, for all that, the fundamental expression of God's power and wisdom:

" . . . Christ crucified, a stumbling block to Jews and fool-
ishness to Gentiles, but to those who are the called, both
Jews and Greeks, Christ the power of God and the wisdom of God."[2]

The fulfillment of the divine weakness in the Incarnation is
demonstrated in a manner that any self-respecting practitioner
of public relations would scorn. Few supernatural trappings
attend the promotional effort. The appeal is directed to the
dregs of society, not the rich and influential. Its persuasions
carry none of the flashy fervor of religious hucksterism. Indeed,
God's effort to cement a bond of love with his lovelorn creatures is one of self-abasement, as dramatically illustrated in
Holman Hunt's famous painting that depicts Christ humbly
seeking admission at the door of a cottage, representing the
human heart. He stands patiently outside without any assurance that his gentle rappings might provoke obscenities, an
object hurled through the window, or, worse, no response at all.

Encounterer (God) Conceals Strengths

The *concealment* of the divine strengths seems fundamental to
the biblical understanding of God. As previously stated, faith
consists in part of the belief that one is obliged to deal with a
Deus absconditus (hidden God). To assert or pretend otherwise is
to make an unfaithful response. Truly, "a religion which does
not affirm that God is hidden is not true."[3]

In this regard we have suggested that the hiddenness of
God in some measure indicates a divine disinclination to interfere with the unfettered choice that authentic love requires.
However ardent the wooer, there can be no arm-twisting a "yes"
from the object of his desire. Compulsion earns hate, not love.
For God to create a race of creatures capable of a relationship of
love requires the option of "no." The freedom that allows for
rejection provides the only conditions that make love a possibility. The point sheds light on a comment reputedly made by
English historian Lord Acton to the effect that God so loved
freedom that he permitted even sin in order to secure it.

God's love, by the scriptural account, makes its approach
clad in the rags of weaknesses. Paul seemed the first to compre-

hend this sublime ambivalence by stating that the humility of that love is, in reality, a demonstration of strength far greater than any divine tyranny. His rhetorical tour de force in 1 Corinthians must be savored in full:

> For Jews demand signs and Greeks desire wisdom, but we proclaim Christ crucified, a stumbling block to Jews and foolishness to Gentiles, but to those who are the called, both Jews and Greeks, Christ the power of God and the wisdom of God. For God's foolishness is wiser than human wisdom, and God's weakness is stronger than human strength. Consider your own call, brothers and sisters: not many of you were wise by human standards, not many were powerful, not many were of noble birth. But God chose what is foolish in the world to shame the wise; God chose what is weak in the world to shame the strong; God chose what is low and despised in the world, things that are not, to reduce to nothing things that are, so that no one might boast in the presence of God.[4]

This weakness of God, the most profound paradox of all, is given poignant expression in the relative clause of the Collect for the eleventh Sunday after Trinity: "O God, who declarest thy almighty power chiefly in showing mercy and pity. . . ."

Encountered's (Humanity's) Weaknesses Are Addressed

According to Scriptures, God's "weaknesses" are directed toward human weaknesses. It is our vulnerability that serves as the target of the divine quest.

Again, the *location* of the divine-human rendezvous requires that humans both recognize and admit weaknesses if they are truly to fall into divine Love. Ramparts of proudful self-sufficiency must be abandoned. One must venture out onto the terrain of Love's demonstrated weaknesses—which to the Christian will be Golgotha, the site of the Crucifixion—and there raise the white flag of one's true status. Only under the conditions of admitted weaknesses, declare the Scriptures, can the power in God's weaknesses become unleashed.

The point lends light to Jesus' puzzling requirement that those seeking his healing powers should actually verbalize the nature of their request, obvious though it be. Thus blind Bartimaeus was made to state a need that could hardly have been more evident:

Then Jesus said to him, "What do you want me to do for you?" The blind man said to him, "My teacher, let me see again." Jesus said to him, "Go; your faith has made you well."[5]

Accordingly, an informed acknowledgment of personal frailty is how engagement with the divine weaknesses begins. By contrast, the Bible vigorously repudiates any suggestion that the heavenly initiative is directed toward such human strengths as intellect, aesthetic sensibilities, or imagination. Indeed, these attributes are regarded more as a barrier to the divine outreach than a means of access. They are but god-like endowments that tempt humans to self-idolatry and rebellion.

The Radical Equality in Human Weaknesses

Scripture does not fail to recognize the relentless human compulsion to seize on God's strengths by means of human strengths. The enticing possibility of commanding the divine powers through spiritual or intellectual forays keeps returning, virus-like, to challenge the Church's tradition of "grace alone."

Long before the New Testament was compiled, so-called gnostic sects had begun to recast the gospel in a manner that suggested that Jesus' mission was one of interaction with human perceptions. His was the task of imparting a higher and secret "wisdom" to those intellectually capable of perceiving its truths and practicing its arcane rituals. The result was a pseudo-Christian religion composed largely of initiates with sufficient leisure and means to pursue a sort of theological dandyism.

A virus still, gnosticism continues to flare both within and without the Church in a variety of forms—"new age" religion and Rosicrucianism being conspicuous examples. Cults, too, with their claim to special information, may be lumped under the general category of gnosticism.

For all their power of durability, gnostic assumptions about the nature of God and humanity must be regarded as deficient for a number of reasons, among them the suggestion of an elitist deity that disdains the great majority of humanity while showing favor to those with sufficient imagination to pierce the divine mystery. Of its nature, such a god would be worthy of scorn, not fidelity and love.

By repudiating gnosticism, biblical faith declares a radical equality among humans on the basis of shared weaknesses and the subsequent universal need for salvation. All humans are united by the bonds of weakness, just as they are divided by individual strengths. Even the unbalanced and retarded stand on an equal footing with all others as far as their potential relationship to God is concerned, for the motions of grace apply universally to frailties, not that lottery of genes and circumstances that result in personalized strengths. Indeed, it could be argued that one finds in Scripture a reverse discrimination policy with its inference that the weakest, by worldly standards, tend to be those for whom grace proves most available. Not the poor and simple but rather the intellectually and economically privileged are in greatest danger of overlooking "the one thing needful."

Thus it is that God's guaranteed approach treads the pathways of human sorrow, pain, hopelessness, and death. He comes to stand alongside those who "sit in darkness and the shadow of death."[6] As one who "knoweth our frame" and remembers that "we are but dust,"[7] the Bible assures us that he makes his approach not by schemes of enlightenment but by means of a cross driven as a claim-stake into the Golgotha of human weakness.

Encountered's (Humanity's) Strengths Are Disregarded

If there is an impassable barrier to the divine encounter, it is the scriptural God's adamant refusal to deal with humans on the basis of presumed strengths. The Psalmist declares: "Though the Lord is high, he regards the lowly, but the haughty he perceives from far away."[8] Innate human arrogance is "an abomination to the Lord,"[9] since "God opposes

the proud, but gives grace to the humble."[10] Thus God's res-
olute absence can be counted on by those who rely on their
wealth[11], wisdom[12], might[13], horses[14], chariots[15], physical
endowments[16], armaments[17], fortifications[18], foreign alliances[19],
family connections[20], religious elitism[21].

To place confidence in human strengths merely blinds one to
the parallel of God's inherent humility in coming to Earth—
with all of its attendant miseries. Intellect and imagination can
serve us only after they have been laid aside in our quest for the
divine. These two faculties play a subservient, postrepentant
role. Only after our disavowal of self-sufficiency, and our admission of guilt and helplessness, can we, according to Scriptures,
apply human strengths at a higher level.

Human Weaknesses as a Proof of God's Existence

The necessity for disarming the power of the intellect in the
quest for God has been given a philosophical dimension by
Karl Barth in his profound study entitled *Anselm: Fides Quaerens
Intellectum.*[22] Anselm was a medieval prelate and scholar who
had long and prayerfully considered the various arguments for
the existence of God that were so popular in his day. Unsat-
isfied, he sought and was given, as he believed, an insight of
divine origin—an argument for God's existence that found its
basis in human weakness; to wit, humankind's intellectual limitations. His famous ontological argument was the result:
"There is something whose non-existence is inconceivable, and
this must be greater than that whose non-existence is conceiv-
able . . . and this thing art thou, O Lord our God."

Anselm's "proof" came to be discounted on the basis that
the capacity to imagine a thing with the mind, even a state of
nonexistence, did not necessarily posit its reality. But in the era
of continental liberalism's bankruptcy following World War I,
Barth resurrected Anselm's insight, suggesting that the critics
failed to grasp the profound intuition that the very limits of
human intelligence provided a clue, albeit negative, to God's
existence. "Man," wrote Barth, "could conceive of nothing . . .
beyond God without lapsing into the . . . absurdity of placing
himself above God in attempting to conceive of this greater."[23]

Barth's conclusion followed that of Pascal, Anselm, Augustine, Paul, and many of the other great minds of Christian history in their collective belief that all attempts to "prove" God could only be resolved by admitting weakness. In the words of Anselm's *Proslogian:* "I do not seek to understand so that I may believe, but believe that I may understand. For this I know to be true: that unless I first believe I shall not understand." It is only by such admission of human frailty and a corresponding dependency-in-faith that one can unbolt the door to the humble, seeking God—the fear of whom, for all his humility, nevertheless serves as the threshold of true wisdom.

Here we reach the culmination of our argument. Cognizance of personal weakness is essential to:

1. Knowledge of self;
2. Knowledge of and interaction with others;
3. A relationship with the God who encounters us only at the level of our weaknesses.

Revising The Encounters

Before turning to a practical method for discerning those personal weaknesses that so paradoxically can serve as a source of strength,

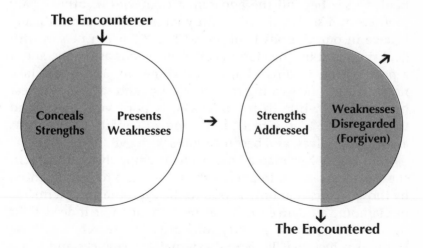

The Ideal Human–Human Encounter (Figure 4)

let us rediagram the human-human, human-divine encounter modes in a manner more consonant with our findings.

In Figure 4 we have altered the human-human encounter in a manner quite opposite that associated with "natural," competitive tendencies. In this mode one does not lead with strengths. Rather personal weaknesses, discerned and admitted, are set to the fore. Further, these are directed toward the encountered's *strengths,* not weaknesses. Gone is the instinctual urge to achieve competitive superiority, with its inevitable derogation and invitation to strife.

The dynamics may be described simply as *humility.* One's weaknesses are acknowledged openly and good-humoredly while one's assets are simultaneously concealed—again recognizing that all display of talents, possessions, connections, and attainments merely invites competitiveness.

As for the weaknesses of others, these will be discerned as well as discounted. Using a more traditional term, they are *forgiven.* Rather, one searches *for* the other's strengths. Of necessity, however, these must be *genuine* strengths, not imposters, inasmuch as the flattering of illusion only feeds weaknesses.

The strengths being addressed should not be those of a superficial nature, such as physical beauty or the trappings of power, influence, and wealth. The Epistle of James implies that one's own weaknesses provide the reason why we find it so difficult to see beyond the apparent weaknesses of others: "My brothers and sisters, do you with your acts of favoritism really believe in our glorious Lord Jesus Christ? For if a person with gold rings and in fine clothes comes into your assembly, and if a poor person in dirty clothes also comes in, and if you take notice of the one wearing the fine clothes and say, 'Have a seat here, please' while to the one who is poor you say, 'Stand there,' or 'Sit at my feet,' have you not made distinctions among yourselves, and become judges with evil thoughts?"[24]

John Henry Newman advises us to attempt always to discern the *soul* in the other. Implied is the resolve not to be influenced by those factors that only appeal to the eye—the accouterments of glamour, affluence, or social prominence nor indeed their opposite: deformity, poverty, obscurity. To search out those spiritual values that lie *behind* external appearances and to do so out of a dispassionate concern (*agape*) for the encountered is to invite shalom.

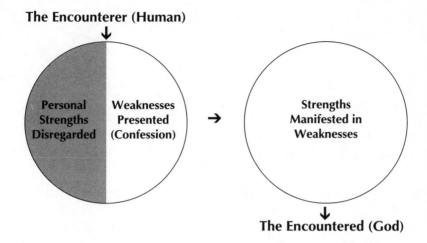

The Encounterer (Human)

Personal
Strengths
Disregarded

Weaknesses
Presented
(Confession)

→

Strengths
Manifested in
Weaknesses

The Encountered (God)

The Ideal Human–Divine Encounter (Figure 5)

As to that ultimate reality for which we use the term *God,* a sense of human limitations generally and personal weaknesses specifically can open the self to unimaginable possibilities. One ordinarily begins the inner journey by allowing at least the *possibility* of what might be described as God's overwhelmingness to enter; that is, his sovereignty, creatorship, unfathomable essence. From there one may even go on to delight in those subtleties of divine strengths that pose as weaknesses: love, mercy, compassion, divine suffering. It is at the level of the quixotic ambivalences of heaven that one is prompted to cry with the Psalmist: "O God, my heart is ready, my heart is ready."[25]

In suggesting these alternative approaches, we are once more made aware of the importance of discerning personal weaknesses for their momentous influence upon our orientation toward others and the eternal. Nor can we overlook the elusiveness of those weaknesses, the extent to which they remain concealed from *ourselves,* tucked behind, as they are, a jerry-built stage set of illusion and self-deception. Thus the urgency with which we now turn to a simple, practical means of discerning those personal weaknesses that so fray our lives.

PRINCIPLE

A Significant Step Toward the Fulfillment of the Self Can Be Achieved through a Systematic, Self-administered Cataloging of Personal Weaknesses

How often have you heard it said: "So and so could be a perfectly wonderful person if it weren't for————"? The rest of the sentence is filled in with a character flaw of some sort or perhaps a bad habit of which the subject seems quite oblivious.

Consider then, for a moment, the possibility that *you yourself* might be the object of such a remark. Your friends see in you all sorts of splendid possibilities but cannot understand why you fail to see "the one thing needful" that is holding you back.

If someone could speak plainly to you without fear of hurting your feelings or causing a rupture in the friendship, what entirely redeemable faults might be mentioned? Could it be something so minor as an unkempt appearance, an annoying habit, an irritating mannerism that, with recognition, could be readily altered?

Ordinarily, we cannot depend upon our friends for the disclosure of our weaknesses. Just as we ourselves are reluctant to point out *their* liabilities, so they deal with us the same way. Even as we tend to resent incoming criticism, however well-intentioned, so we rein in our evaluation of others, knowing that those who divulge truths about their friends "for their own good" usually do not remain friends for long.

Even wives and husbands are disinclined to point out each other's faults, though surely this is one of marriage's responsibilities, inasmuch as a touch of iodine, lovingly administered, may be all that is required for healing. Nevertheless, spouses neglect truth-telling about such amendable conditions as bad breath, conversation monopolization, maliciousness, and over-imbibing to the extent of underscoring a central affirmation of this book: namely, that the only one truly capable of uncovering personal weaknesses is the possessor.

Responsibility for the Self Belongs to the Self

Responsibility for the self, after all, belongs to the self. No one outside an individual's personal borders can (or should) be delegated those obligations that are properly those of the self alone. In affirming such an axiomatic truth, we would add that every person not only has the responsibility to discover the truth about himself or herself but also possesses the necessary instruments. Self-transcendence is, after all, a distinguishing characteristic of the human race.

Indeed we can go further. Each of us is better equipped, better qualified on this matter than anyone else. Such fundamental questions as Who am I? What is my condition? What am I to do? What am I to make of this mysterious existence into which I have been thrown?—these can receive their only satisfactory answers from the self alone.

This is not to say that there are never occasions when external help is required in dealing with life's imponderables. But the final resolution returns home, the alternatives being either a debilitating dependency on others or the fool's world of assumptions and illusions—either option being disastrous.

Self-reliance in the healing process is hardly fashionable nowadays. Blathering seems to be the therapy of choice, as we are encouraged to seek advice from as many as we can persuade or afford: physicians, counselors, clergy, psychiatrists, support groups, and so forth. As in so many areas of modern life, people are driven sheeplike—in this instance by the dubious proposition that not only the source of life's problems but also the solution lies outside the self.

Overlooked in today's counseling frenzy are some fairly cru-cial issues, beginning with the liabilities that attend abdication of the self's autonomy. Must we be content to assume, for example, that the dependencies associated with psychotherapy necessarily provide a satisfactory alternative to emotional dys-function? At very least, the transference phenomenon ("You be my parent and tell me what to do") raises ethical concerns. Who can estimate the number of therapy-dependent zombies walking our streets who find themselves unable to make the most minor decision without consulting their support net-works? One finds in their plight the haunting question of mod-ern psychology: namely, to what extent can self-autonomy, once yielded, be fully recovered?

At the same time, we might also observe that the deeply-rooted human tendency to relinquish responsibility for the self seems matched by the readiness of others to assume it. Thus we experience the common incongruity of the counselor whose own life is in shambles even as he or she zealously directs the lives of his or her clients.

Ironic too is the fact that while much current therapy centers on the issue of *control,* there remains a general blindness to its pervasive presence in the therapeutic process itself. A woman told me that after years of attending Alcoholics Anonymous, together with a related support group and a one-on-one coun-selor, she began to feel enmeshed in repetitious talk, conclud-ing it was time to strike out in new directions. When she announced her decision, she was met by a barrage of strident objections to the effect that members of the *group,* not she, were the ones to decide whether or not she was ready to leave.

The crisis resolved itself into a revelation. The woman recog-nized, as never before, the extent to which her life had been marked by the surrender of autonomy—to her father, to her husband, to her bosses, and now to her psychological coun-selors and peers. Later she confided that the greatest moment of her years in therapy came with the liberating "No!" that ended the sessions.

Other liabilities come to mind. Some have suggested that group therapy can have the effect of *enhancing* inappropriate illusions, making contact with the true self all the more diffi-cult. The support group junkie who spends most evenings of the

week airing his or her innermost thoughts may be in reality pol-
ishing a false *persona* before a captive audience, with the result
that the authentic self, far from being strengthened and liber-
ated, becomes increasingly submerged. The lust for sympathetic
listening can readily sabotage so-called group dynamics, a fact
that may account for the anomaly that support groups intended
to cure addictive behavior can themselves turn into addiction.

The raising of these concerns is not intended to call into
question the usefulness of individual or group therapy, but
rather to indicate the possibility of other avenues toward the
fulfillment of the self among its own. The unassisted self is
admittedly a feeble thing. But let us never submit to the proposition that it is *helpless*.

In contemplating the dichotomy between other-directed and
inner-directed therapy, we must now turn to some questions
frequently asked about the Personal Weaknesses Inventory.

*Given the complexity of the human personality, is it not sim-
plistic to suggest that the assembly of Personal Weaknesses
Inventory can, in and of itself, bring about significant therapeutic benefits?*

Certainly no one in the psychological field would deny that
whenever hitherto unrecognized factors in a life are given cognitive identification, change is bound to occur. Simple or sim-
plistic, the act of confronting life's debilities will be beneficial if
for no other reason than that contained in Freud's dictum:
"Where there was id, let there be ego."

*People spend untold hours in various forms of psychotherapy.
Do you mean to suggest that the relatively brief period envi-
sioned by the Personal Weaknesses Inventory can provide
comparable results?*

Comparison here is impossible. The Inventory assumes an investment of about fifteen minutes per day over a period of six
weeks. Its objective is an unadorned listing of perceived weaknesses. There is but a cursory effort to ferret out the *source* of
these weaknesses, as would be the object of most therapies.

There are those who probably believe that only limited benefits would come of such a procedure, but at least we can agree

that a new openness to transformation of the self might encourage some to seek psychotherapy as a logical extension of the Inventory. An additional dividend would be the reduction of resistance to therapy's necessary assault upon the ego's defenses.

Whether or not augmented by therapy, the Inventory will have an impact, in some cases dramatic, upon those who conscientiously carry the program through to completion. A "cure" for one's emotional ills is by no means promised. Rather what is assured is "the beginning of a beginning," which is to say the commencement of a lifelong habit of realistic self-assessment in the spirit of the Delphic principle, "know thyself." Of its very nature, such openness to life's realities will prove a far more powerful element in the transformation of the self than may be supposed.

Can a self-administered Personal Weaknesses Inventory adequately confront the human capacity for self-deception?

That we lie to ourselves often and effectively cannot be denied. We have already noted how early in the life cycle humans contrive a "personage," then become its first and most uncritical believers. It is such self-deception that makes us so vulnerable to the blandishments of positive thinkers with their suggestion that our facades can become our homes. Kierkegaard said of Hegel's philosophy that while it may have been a castle of thought, one was nevertheless compelled to live in reality's hut by its side. So it is with the personage we construct. The capacity to "undeceive" ourselves about its illusions does not come easily, but once the first fruits have been gathered the incentive to proceed is irresistible.

Moreover, we are bound to ask what possible alternatives to realistic self-assessment can there be? After all, there is not a mother's son or daughter of us who is not, to some degree, incapacitated by inner flaws. Some may have been visited upon us. Others may be of our own devising. Surely no good comes of remaining oblivious to them, inasmuch as they constitute a threat to our health, our careers, our talents, our vocation, our relationships, our marriages, and our children.

As is commonly known, the word *sin* means "missing the mark." Could it not be said that weaknesses undiscovered, and unacknowledged, are our true sins, preventing, as they do, acceleration and direction toward life's goals? Who would not gladly appropriate the promise of the Army television commercial to "be all that you can be"? However, like the thugs they are, our weaknesses stalk us from the darkness, conferring upon us unhappiness, loneliness, depression, nonproductivity, unhealthy dependencies, anxieties, and worse.

The moment we recognize our personal weaknesses for what they are, the moment we understand the extent and power of them, the moment we realize the influence they hold over our lives and destiny, we can begin to take hold of the necessary antidote to self-deception. Inner integrity, however painful, emerges as the only alternative, thus enabling us to come to terms with these adversaries, to dismiss them for their inability to provide appropriate defenses, and to be done with their false promises, illusions, and delusions forever.

Is not the creation of a Personal Weaknesses Inventory a threat to those who exist on the emotional margins of life?

The question reminds me of the middle-aged woman who told me she had never attended a funeral, never viewed a corpse. The problem was not the sight of a lifeless body itself but rather the ego's fear that it might become emotionally overwhelmed. The rational response here is that phobic fears of all sorts—corpses, snakes, spiders, enclosed places, flying—are best dealt with by confrontation.

Without doubt, a significant degree of anxiety will attend any in-depth assessment of the self. One person to whom I proposed the Inventory literally ran from the room, calling over her shoulder, "I know my weaknesses! And if there are others, I don't want to know about them!" The remark was revealing for several reasons: first, its instinctive protection of the personage; second, its dubious assumption that whatever undiscovered flaws might be perceived and acknowledged would prove so horrible that there would be no coping with them. Again, we say that the only effectual cure for indeterminate anxiety is a level look at the corpse.

The issue of determining another person's ability to cope with methodical self-scrutiny also raises an ethical issue; namely, who has the right to determine what may be right or wrong for oneself? My experience in pastoral counseling has led me to believe that even in cases of deep emotional disturbance the capacity of the self to deal both realistically and compassionately with its inner makeup is far greater than commonly assumed. Let individuals fully understand the difference between self-analysis and self-accusation, let them understand that an inventory of weaknesses is not to be regarded as a list of reproaches assembled by an internalized parent with condemnation to follow, let them acknowledge repressed and unpleasant data about themselves, and more than likely they will experience not greater anxiety but rather a profound relief.

We do not suggest that a frank assessment of one's weaknesses will be free of hazards. Like Childe Roland, the person who dares such a venture will find the approach to the dark tower that conceals the hidden self at once fearful and necessary. Again we must ask, What options remain? Are they not, one and all, more ominous still? And even if some must approach the dark tower more cautiously than others, creeping from one defensive redoubt to another, who is to say that the goal cannot at last be achieved?

I am reminded of two members of a parish I formerly served who were oppressed by various emotional demons. When first encountered, both were floundering in an effort to bolster fragile self-identities with presumed strengths, which in general could be described as the illusion of being the source of great and original thoughts that were destined to change the world.

Each was gently urged by me and others to examine these illusory strengths, even as they owned up to the fact that they presently lay in the grip of debilitating psychoses. One fiercely resisted our suggestions, leaving us to stand by and watch as she gradually sank into a netherworld of total mental chaos. The other, however, with a courage which amazed all, began to see that the illusion of being more creative, more gifted, more promising than everyone else was not only untrue, but destructive. Gradually, he was able to wean himself from these false self-assurances to the point that he discovered some of his genuine strengths and thereby was enabled to reenter society on a basis that was acceptable to all concerned. In retrospect, I find him one of the most admirable persons I have ever met.

Could you identify or characterize the dynamics for change associated with a Personal Weaknesses Inventory?

The energy to be gained from an analysis of personal weaknesses derives primarily from a shift in perspective on the self. For this change in orientation I have coined the word *reperspective,* which is to say a different outlook upon the self.

The inherent power of reperspective can be nuclear, as may be observed in such common experiences as religious conversion or falling in love. In either case, the desire of the subject to connect with the object of its longing induces a process of self-observation from the other's perspective. Seeing the self through the beloved's eyes has the power of causing an almost instantaneous transformation.

Experienced in a religious dimension, one views the self from the perspective of the righteous God. As described in William James's *Varieties of Religious Experience* and elsewhere, the experience can bring about immediate reformation. Individuals discern as never before the flaws and blemishes that alienate them from the source of their being. That upheaval in personal behavior—which is theologically described as "repentance"—causes a new self to emerge. One is "born again." Old habits, false values, and inappropriate behavior melt away in a matter of seconds, and a new life is begun.

The conversion phenomenon is often dismissed as episodic. This may be true in a considerable number of instances, but not all. Would anyone deny that at least some hardened substance abusers, predators, derelicts, and criminals have become model citizens almost instantaneously through the power of religious reperspective?

Scriptures tell of the transformation of an arrogant, denying Peter by little more than a fleeting glimpse of himself through his Master's eyes: "the Lord turned and looked upon Peter."[1] One is similarly reminded of a man by the name of John Newton who captured a sudden vision of himself in the guise of a degenerate slaver. The experience was sufficient to transform him into a penitent who could write the words: "Amazing grace, how sweet the sound, that saved a wretch like me."

Falling in love also demonstrates the power of reperspective. Some years ago I was obliged to be in Chicago and arranged to be picked up at O'Hare Airport by a person I'd known virtually all my life. Through the years this person had left the impression upon all who knew him of an untidy, shambling sort of fellow—the sort who, if he shaved at all in the morning, did so without looking; who used a comb composed of no more than three teeth; who attired himself with the topmost item on the pile of clothing that lay in the corner, whatever its color, compatibility, or condition. Always overweight, his stomach seemed indelibly associated in my mind with thread snarls about halfway down his shirt where a button had popped off.

This was the person I was supposed to be meeting. As I stood in the concourse awaiting his arrival (I knew he'd be late), I found myself being approached by someone I assumed was preparing to ask directions. In fact, it was the man who had come to meet me, and I didn't recognize him—was even scanning the crowd when he called me by name. There he stood: straight and slim, with unimaginable poise and self-assurance. His clothing was coordinated and pressed, his shoes polished, his topcoat impeccable, and every last hair on his head positioned perfectly. In bewilderment I heard myself mumbling, "It looks like you've lost a couple of pounds."

I should have guessed at once the cause of this "miracle," though I did not learn the truth of it until we were twenty miles from the airport and nearing our destination. *The man had fallen in love!* And had he changed? Until that time, neither sticks nor staves could have caused him to put polish to shoes. Only here he was, looking like Beau Brummel! All it took was the right woman and with it the capacity to see himself through her eyes. Such is the power of reperspective.

Through the Personal Weaknesses Inventory we will attempt to harness that power by means of a new slant upon the self. Some introductory words and a description of the procedure itself will occupy the concluding chapter.

8

The Personal Weaknesses Inventory

Before describing how the Personal Weaknesses Inventory is undertaken, it will be necessary to set forth three prerequisites. I would ask the reader to peruse these carefully and decide in advance whether or not they can be fulfilled. If not, the wisest course would be to delay the process until more appropriate conditions prevail. The three conditions are:

1. The determination to see the task through to completion;
2. The establishment, as nearly as possible, of an invariable time and place for the daily procedure;
3. Absolute, unrelenting secrecy.

Let us take these requirements one by one and attempt to show why they are so necessary.

1) Seeing It Through.

The procedure, as developed, requires the investment of approximately fifteen minutes per day for a period of six weeks. From the hither side, such an outlay of time may seem a proverbial snap of the finger. Only be advised that by the time the project is brought to completion, it will be regarded as having been an exercise in endurance.

From an ordinary perspective, fifteen minutes is no more than half the time of a typical news telecast. But when it comes to intensive self-scrutiny, those minutes will increasingly begin to resemble centuries.

Why is this so? Because the proceedings will be threatening to the psyche as it perceives an advance being made on forbidden territory. And so, inner alarms will sound as the ego mounts an effort to protect itself from what it considers a hostile campaign against the self.

In the process, the mind will be told to resist, and it will oblige in various ways. It will grow bored, distracted, irritable, incapable of concentration. It will begin to toss out all sorts of plausible reasons why the exercise should be discontinued. "You are wasting your time!" "You've completed as much of this exercise as your personal situation warrants!" "This sort of thing is meant for other people!" "There are more pressing matters at hand!"

These and similar thoughts will tempt many to abandon the Inventory somewhere around the middle of the second week. Be forewarned.

What must be remembered throughout is a fundamental insight of psychotherapy; namely, the closer one comes to the root of emotional dysfunction, the greater the resistance. Accordingly, the capacity of the conscious mind to function efficiently will be diminished. It will lose the capacity for focus. It will become careless.

Here may be found one of the reasons why the participant should be prepared to go over the same ground again and again, so as to insure that no crucial factor has been overlooked. It is as though one were scrutinizing the ground for a key that was inadvertently dropped in the grass. Moving back and forth over the same small patch, inspecting it from every angle and cast of light, even to the point of getting on hands and knees to feel for what the eye cannot see, may prove the only means to a successful conclusion. In such cases, the slapdash approach simply will not do.

2) Establish a Regular Time Each Day for the Project.

Unless a specific portion of time for each day is set aside in advance, the assembly of an Inventory is apt to be delayed until late at night, often the last remaining minutes before retiring. Such is a typical unconscious maneuver for avoiding the odious—and, once again, uncovering personal weaknesses *will* have its odious side. When work on the Inventory is left to the waning moments of the day, one is further tempted to salve the conscience with the vague promise of a double-dose effort in the morning. There is no need to rehearse the melancholy possibilities here.

The chosen time of day should consider the amount of concentration required. For some, the Inventory will best be undertaken in the morning before the house is stirring. For others, either a lunch break or an after-dinner routine will prove more convenient. One must apply careful and imaginative forethought to time and place. A private nook at home, a park bench, a public library, the atrium of an office building, or simply a shut door with an implicit or explicit "do not disturb" message provide various possibilities. The adoption of an invariable time and place should take into consideration, too, the privacy factor. A furtive or secretive approach will only entice curiosity. Since outright deception is not recommended, judicious planning is necessary.

3) *Maintain Absolute Secrecy.*

Of absolute, of *crucial* importance is the resolve to keep all aspects of the Inventory private—before, during, and after the procedure. Determine in advance that neither your project nor its results will ever be revealed to anyone. When you have completed your work, destroy all written materials, and throttle the temptation to discuss your endeavors. The reason? If at any time during the exercise you so much as anticipate revealing your efforts or their findings, blocking mechanisms designed to protect the ego will automatically be triggered. The result may well be a catalog of worthless pseudo-weaknesses more intended to create an impression than target the truth.

Transformation of the self can only come when truth is given absolute precedence over all else, the personage most of all. The self must be allowed to rise alone in majestic isolation as it examines the particularities of its condition. Total confidentiality is the only means of assuring as much.

These preliminary considerations form a *sine qua non* for the successful completion of this work. If carried forward faithfully, the Personal Weaknesses Inventory will almost certainly change the life of its subject for the better, perhaps dramatically so.

We turn now to the Inventory itself. Four steps are required.

Preparing a Personal Weaknesses Inventory

Step 1: The Comprehensive List
(Weeks 1 through 3)

Having established a consistent time and place for the project, begin by listing on a pad of paper those aspects of your life that you deem to be personal weaknesses. Proceed in a random, stream-of-consciousness manner. Use either words or phrases. Do not attempt to account for these weaknesses. Initially, what is required is simply a list with no explanation or rationalization whatsoever. In the process consider three general areas.

Handicaps. The term is used here to describe those liabilities of life for which you are not primarily responsible. Include inherent disorders, maladies, sexual maladjustments, disabilities, adverse circumstances. While some handicaps may be recent acquisitions, the great majority will be inherited—congenital deformities, proneness to various ailments or disorders, flawed vision or hearing, family tendencies toward such conditions as heart disease, diabetes, obesity, and physical or emotional debilities. Circumstances of birth should also be considered weaknesses and are to be frankly acknowledged: illegitimacy, minority status, abandonment to foster care, and so forth. Add weaknesses imposed by the adverse influences of earliest childhood: stressful environment, inadequate nourishment, discord between parents or absent parents, addictive behavior in the home, family dysfunction, parental ignorance or emotional instability, habitual breach of promise, neglect, severe or arbitrary punishment, capricious change of parental mood, sexual abuse by parents or other adults or peers, trauma, undue parental strictness or, alternately, indulgence. Note, while listing such liabilities, subtle societal discrimination warrants that your age be included as a handicap if you are under eighteen or over forty-five. Add also a fair estimate of your personal attractiveness and innate intelligence.

Encumbrances. This term denotes those liabilities, past and present, for which *you yourself* are responsible: bad decisions, missed opportunities, betrayals, failure in school or employment, financial setbacks, bad or dissolved marriages, sexual promiscuity, public disgrace, indebtedness, bankruptcy, flawed reputation, prevarications, misrepresentations, felonies, misde-meanors, prison records, harm inflicted on self or others by poor judgment, episodes of intoxication, and so forth.

Tendencies and Bad Habits. The list should also include more commonly regarded human weaknesses, which is to say those tendencies and bad habits that bring out the worst in us. In my own personal Inventory I listed over fifty such weaknesses from belligerence to laziness. As one proceeds, new areas of consideration will come to mind without conscious effort and are apt to do so at any time. For example, halfway to the post office one morning, I suddenly became aware how much the forces of impatience, fretfulness, and worry oppressed me. At my next session I began to explore a whole new region of debilities.

Step 2: Delineation and Compression
(Week 4)

Starting with the fourth week, you can begin a period of evaluation and refinement. By this time the list of weaknesses may extend into the hundreds. What is needed is a process of distillation by which the list is reduced to a manageable size. For example, the same weakness may be described variously. Determine what describes the situation most accurately, and cull out the rest. Eliminate those weaknesses that seem less important than others or are derivative. At the same time be alert to the self-deceptive tendency to concentrate on trivial weaknesses at the expense of the truly massive ones.

As the development of the "short list" proceeds, use this week to consider the following question more candidly than ever before: "What weaknesses do *others* perceive in me?" Do your best to regard yourself realistically through the eyes of family, friends—yes, and even strangers. Understand that few of them admire you unreservedly; but, by the same standard, few despise you. Be aware that, as noted in chapter 2, their basic attitude toward you will be governed by your weaknesses.

As you proceed to add third-person observations to your previous listing, consider also how they correlate with your own self-examination. For example, if you feel others regard you as stuck-up or aloof, you may have already listed such weaknesses as a prevailing distrust or fear of other people. The relationship between two such factors will be obvious.

**Step 3: Processing Your Findings
(Week 5)**

Required now is a supply of paper (a lined, yellow, legal-sized pad will do). With a ruler, draw two vertical lines, leaving three columns. Head column 1 "Weaknesses," column 2 "Source/ Analysis," and column 3 "Transformation." Week 5 will be concentrated on columns 1 and 2.

Under "Weaknesses," enter your final list, leaving three or four spaces between each entry. Then for the remainder of the week, begin a series of reflective sessions in which you attempt a realistic discernment of the *source* of the weaknesses you have listed. Most will be evident enough, but a few may require some delving into memories, many of them painful. Press on with courage, for pain is ordinarily the prelude to healing. Analysis will invariably accompany this aspect of the Inventory, but caution is urged against the sort of analysis that translates into rationalizations. The idea is *not* to find reasons why you are the way you are—which, with the proverbial nickel, may get you a cup of coffee. Rather, seek a thoroughly reliable estimate of the self, so that the energies of reperspective can provide the wherewithal of positive transformation.

Understand that there is no "correct" source to any given weakness. A similar failing by various persons may have emerged from entirely different circumstances. For example, episodic rage might be perceived by one as deriving from a specific childhood trauma, by another from severe parental repression, and by yet another from the acquired realization that "rage works." Analyze the possibilities your conscious mind suggests, and select the most compelling. Do not be surprised at the degree of repression that can accompany the exercise. In considering my own experience with the Inventory some years ago, I recall that the search for the source of my weaknesses led to bouts of overwhelming sleepiness, indeed to the point of falling asleep while seated upright in my office chair. As soon as I recognized this as emblematic of a powerful inner resistance to disturbing old scars, the symptom disappeared.

**Step 4: Transformation
(Week 6)**

If listing and refining of personal weaknesses in Steps 1 and 2 were the sum of the Inventory, one might conclude that it offered little more than another exercise in introspection. To conclude with Step 3, and its attempt to identify the source of personal weaknesses, leaves one with little more than self-exoneration—that is, "the devil made me do it!" Here, incidentally, may be found another limitation of support group therapy with its emphasis on source and analysis. A perpetual discussion on the issue of "What made me the way I am?" can leave one paralyzed by introspection, incapable of accepting the power of transforming grace. Many go through life bitterly accusing parents for their failures without realizing that by doing so they abdicate responsibility for the present source of their difficulties, namely, the self. With the Personal Weaknesses Inventory, self-responsibility is all. One must convince oneself that parental influence no longer determines the future. The "good" parents can be appropriated with thanks, even as the "bad" can be transformed into the good; that is, if we identify and acknowledge its effects on our lives and take responsibility for its metamorphosis into something positive. The potentialities being described here belong to the self alone. Such an understanding enables one to exchange blame for forgiveness and allows forgiveness to open the way to a new life altogether.

In the "Transformation" column, begin to list *practical* means by which the weaknesses that have been listed can be converted to strengths. Do so boldly, with the conviction that the most long-standing, deeply-rooted frailties can be reformulated as assets in life. For example, irrational bouts of anger can yield to a detached, even humorous response to the goads that assail our sensitivities, if we make ourselves aware of the hidden weaknesses at work. Again, inappropriate sexual behavior can be changed from a destructive mode to the *constructive*, once its nature and consequences are recognized. Such tendencies as procrastination or garrulousness will yield to positive social behavior if clearly discerned. Yes, even "age, ache, penury, and imprisonment"—to borrow a phrase from no less than William Shakespeare—have their rewards, once their liabilities are admitted.

The transformation of the greater portion of personal weaknesses will require the breaking of habits—habitual ways of thinking, reacting, behaving. As resistant as bad habits may seem, they too are amenable to change once their total impact on life is elevated into consciousness. We might recall, for example, the success of such programs as cognitive intervention in dealing with those habitual behaviors that lend themselves to clinical depression.

As sweeping as these reassurances may seem, they should not be construed as a superficial solution to extraordinarily complex problems. We too regard with awe the imponderabilities of the human condition. Nevertheless we maintain the validity of our central conviction: namely, that through systematic identification and acknowledgment of personal weaknesses, whatever their source, one becomes open to those enablements by which weaknesses can be converted to genuine strengths.

The process is initiated by the dynamics of *confession* in its truest and most compelling form; that is, a comprehensive awareness of the truth about oneself along with the acknowledgment of that truth to self, to others, and to high heaven. The momentum generated by such a beginning propels one into the realms of repentance, which is to say the reordering of life. Assisted by the catalyst of reperspective, it is the most powerful means of personal change that exists.

With the conclusion of Week 6, the process does not end. By now the detection of inner liabilities will have become a way of life, leading one "from strength to strength." As the years pass, one will be able to look back and view from afar the fool's world of false illusions.

To be sure, there will come times when present realities may tempt one back into the security of denying weaknesses and magnifying presumed strengths. But the temptation will be momentary, as one realizes that the choice lies between a meandering path to nowhere and the narrow, demanding road of life abundant that ascends ever upward, a bracing wind in one's face.

Notes

Introduction

1. Aileen Ward, *John Keats: The Making of a Poet* (New York: Viking Press, 1963), 256. Keats's exact comment is as follows: "Conversation is not a search after knowledge but an endeavor at effect."

Chapter 1

1. Many of the seminal ideas for this book were introduced to the author by the writings of the Swiss physician-psychiatrist Paul Tournier. See especially *The Meaning of Persons,* trans. Edwin Hudson (London: SCM Cheap Edition, 1957).

2. Galatians 5:1.

3. Psalm 84:7.

4. "One is neither so happy or unhappy as one imagines." *Bartlett's Dictionary of Quotations,* 2nd ed. (New York: Oxford University Press, 1953), 407.

5. C. S. Lewis, *Surprised By Joy: The Shape of My Early Life* (San Diego: Harvest/HBJ edition, 1956), 226.

6. Tournier, *The Meaning of Persons,* 13. Tournier takes cognizance of the more common persona to indicate the idealized self-projection. He writes, "Professor C. G. Jung uses the Latin word *persona* to express not what we mean by the word 'person', but rather

'personage,' in the sense in which I shall be using it in this book." My indebtedness to Tournier causes me to retain his term.

7. John Updike, *Rabbit at Rest* (New York: Fawcett Crest, 1990), 122. Emphasis mine.

Chapter 2

1. Edgar Lee Masters, *Spoon River Anthology* (New York: Collier Books, 1962), 169.

2. Tracy Everbach, "Man Who Defrauded Airline Is Sentenced," *The Dallas Morning News,* March 27, 1993, 1A.

3. Luke 12:20.

Chapter 3

1. Stanley Kowalski serves as the perfect foil to Blanche DuBois, the poignant, aging Southern belle who labors so strenuously to present her strengths while concealing her weaknesses. Adopting a mask of aristocracy, manners, and aesthetic sensibilities, she refuses to abandon her pretenses, even when they are cruelly exposed by Kowalski, her brother-in-law.

Chapter 4

1. Karen Horney, M.D., *The Neurotic Personality of Our Time* (New York: W. W. Norton, 1937).

2. Horney, *Neurotic Personality,* 235.

3. Matthew 23:13. Freely rendered.

4. Quoted in Tournier, *The Meaning of Persons,* 69.

Chapter 5

1. 2 Corinthians 12:10.

2. Thérèse of Lisieux, *Autobiography of a Saint,* trans. Ronald Knox (London: Fontana Books, 1958), 94. Her exact expression is as follows: "Talking to God, I felt, is always better than talking about God; those pious conversations—there's always a touch of self-approval about them."

3. Most readers will recognize Friedrich Schleiermacher as the nineteenth century "father of modern theology." The quote about "starry" skies and "moral law" is, of course, from the conclusion of Immanuel Kant's *Critique of Practical Reason,* trans. L. W. Beck (Chicago: University of Chicago, 1949). Rudolf Otto's seminal work, *The Idea of the Holy* (trans. J. W. Harvey [New York: Oxford University Press, 1958]), reintroduced the element of God's transcendence into modern theological discussion.

4. Luke 18:2–6.

5. The Arabic term *Islam* literally means "submission."

6. Albert Camus, *The Fall,* trans. Justin O'Brien (London: Hamish Hamilton, 1957), 37.

7. Psalm 94:1 (King James Version).

8. John Fowles, *The Collector* (Boston: Little, Brown & Company, 1963), 239.

9. John Updike, *Self-Consciousness: Memoirs* (New York: Alfred A. Knopf, 1989), 229.

10. Quoted in John Hick, *The Existence of God* (New York: Macmillan, 1964), 17.

11. Samuel Terrien, *The Elusive Presence: Toward a New Biblical Theology* (San Francisco: Harper and Row Publishers, 1978).

12. Fyodor Dostoyevsky, *The Brothers Karamazov,* trans. Constance Garnett (New York: Modern Library, 1977), 254.

13. Deuteronomy 6:5, Matthew 22:31, and elsewhere.

Chapter 6

1. 1 Corinthians 1:27.

2. 1 Corinthians 1:23–24.

3. Terrien, *The Elusive Presence,* frontispiece.

4. 1 Corinthians 1:22–29.

5. Mark 10:51–52.

6. Psalm 107:10 (KJV).

7. Psalm 103:14 (KJV).

8. Psalm 138:6.

9. Proverbs 16:5.

10. Proverbs 3:34, James 4:6, 1 Peter 5:5.

11. Isaiah 45:6.

12. Proverbs 21:30.

13. Jeremiah 9:23.

14. Isaiah 31:1.

15. Isaiah 31:1.

16. Psalm 33:16.

17. Psalm 44:6.

18. Jeremiah 5:17.

19. Jeremiah 46:25.

20. Matthew 3:9.

21. Amos 5:21.

22. Clifford Green, ed., *Karl Barth: Theologian of Freedom* (London: Collins, 1989), 140–47.

23. Green, *Barth,* 146.

24. James 2:1–4.

25. Psalm 108:1. Traditional *Book of Common Prayer* rendering (New York: Church Pension Fund, 1928).

Chapter 7

1. Luke 22:61.

Index